Stabat Mater

Previous Publications

Pope Pius XII and the Jews: An Answer to Hochhuth's Play, Der Stellvertreter, Glen Rock, NJ, Paulist Press, 1963

Archbishop Denis Eugene Hurley, Notre Dame, IN, University of Notre Dame Press, 1965

The Church in Transition, London, Geoffrey Chapman, 1967 and Notre Dame, IN, Fides Publishers, 1967

Broadcasting in Ireland, London, Routledge & Kegan Paul, 1978

The Right to Communicate: Towards a Definition, Paris, UNESCO, 1978

The Right to Communicate: A Status Report, Paris, UNESCO, 1982

Satellite Broadcasting: The Next Opportunity, ed. D. Fisher, London, The Economist and International Institute of Communications, 1982

The Right to Communicate: A New Human Right, eds. Desmond Fisher and L. S. Harms, Dublin, Boole Press, 1983

Stabat Mater
The Mystery Hymn

Desmond Fisher

GRACEWING

First published in England in 2015
by
Gracewing
2 Southern Avenue
Leominster
Herefordshire HR6 0QF
United Kingdom
www.gracewing.co.uk

ISBN 978 085244 862 5

Typeset by Gracewing

Cover design by Bernardita Peña Hurtado

Dedication

To Peggy, my first and only love, my wife,
my life-long companion and my dearest friend.

CONTENTS

Acknowledgements

HIS BOOK WOULD not have seen the light of day without the encouragement and aid of several people. Foremost among them were two of my children, my youngest son, John, and my daughter Carolyn. It was John who read the earliest drafts and demonstrated a remarkable talent for sub-editing that involved both perceptive comment and the diligent use of a red pen. He also was the technical expert who solved my frequent computer and broadband problems and kept the show on the road.

Special thanks also to my eldest son, Michael, who provided his valuable experience and skills especially at the proof-reading stage. To my grandson, Sam, I am indebted for his expertise when I had problems with my computer and when I thought I had lost several chapters and drafts of the book. Also many thanks to my son Hugh who, by so generously giving of his time in looking after my daily needs, enabled me to concentrate on finishing this book.

Carolyn joined the team in the later stages and used her quick understanding and sharp judgement to modify my tendency to embroider my prose and overstate my criticisms. It was also thanks to her that I was fortunate to get support from an unexpected source.

One of her many friends is Trish Slattery, an American lady living in Dublin. She generously offered to apply her skills as a copy editor and proof reader to reading my manuscript not once but three times, 'initially to get a sense of your writer's voice, then again with a lay person's view for readability and understanding and finally from a proofreader/copyeditor perspective.' Her proposal was gratefully accepted.

I was also fortunate in my next collaborator. Íde Ní Laoghaire, too, is a brilliant copy editor and the former editorial director of one of Ireland's best publishers. Years ago, she and I had worked efficaciously together on copy editing some important new books and I had first hand experience of her wisdom, good judgment and objectivity. She immediately agreed to read my draft, which she did over a weekend, and her subsequent words of advice were invaluable.

My thanks, too, to Mary McGlynn, friend and fellow-Vatican II crusader, for her valuable suggestions and her encouragement.

As far as the content is concerned, most of the research was done on my MacBook laptop. I also depended substantially on a handful of books; the main ones being *The Popes* by John Julius Norwich, *The Catholic Encyclopedia, Jacopone da Todi, poet and mystic* by Evelyn Underhill and *The Fool of God* by George T. Peck.

All of this activity would have been barren without the advice of an old friend and the publisher of one of my earliest publications. She is Sue Chapman, widow of the great Australian publisher, Geoffrey Chapman. It was she who gave me invaluable guidance about the structure and style the book should aim for and who suggested the publisher who accepted it for publication.

Finally, I am very grateful to Tom Longford of Gracewing, my publishers, for his skilful and considerate guidance of a nonagenarian writer through the pre-publication processes.

To all of you my sincere thanks.

INTRODUCTION

HE *STABAT MATER* is one of the best known of the many hymns in the liturgical riches of the Roman Catholic Church. Catholics have recited it for over six hundred years since it began to circulate in central Italy in the late fourteenth century. It then spread throughout large parts of Europe and was translated into many different languages and put to music by several composers. It is now known throughout the worldwide Catholic Church as one of the hymns recited or sung on those occasions in the liturgical year especially devoted to Mary, the mother of Christ.

Despite its popularity, the basic details about the poem are still largely unknown. Who the composer was is disputed. When and where the hymn was first written is uncertain. There are different versions of the original text with some slight variations between them. The purpose for which it was written is undetermined. And it is anyone's guess why a hymn that started out as a commonplace folksong, became associated with the deaths of thousands of people and subsequently banned by the Council of Trent finally became so popular and so highly esteemed.

It is unlikely, though not impossible, that these obscurities will ever be fully clarified. So conclusions about the identity of the author, his motives for writing the poem, why he chose the format he did and what effect he intended it to produce must necessarily be conjecture.

However, conjecture based on reasonable deductions from the known facts and on further study of the poem itself can throw fresh light on the *Stabat Mater* mysteries. This is what is offered here.

Some readers might justifiably question the need for a new translation of a poem that is so widely known throughout the Roman Catholic world. At last count, there were several hundred prose translations, sixty or more of them in English, four well-known English poetry translations, several others that could not really be classified as poetry, as well as some four hundred musical versions of it in existence. Why another?

One answer might be that, if so many people have been competing to make new versions of it, there must be something important and challenging about it. If they are still doing so, it is logical to conclude that the definitive English poetry version has still to be found.

This book is the latest challenger for that distinction. The justification for it is that it claims to be more accurate than the previous ones. By more accurate it is meant that this new version:

- translates the original Latin into English more faithfully than the existing ones;
- uses the same metric and rhyming arrangements as the original throughout, whereas other translations do not do so consistently or at all;
- more faithfully reproduces the emotional mood of the original Latin hymn and, therefore,
- more authentically identifies the purpose for which the poem was written.

Admittedly, these are blanket claims that require substantiation. As with the pudding, the proof is in the consumption. That requires the proof-seeker to turn to the end section of this book where my new translation is given as well as explanations of the hows and whys a particular word or phrase was chosen.

Also included and compared against my own version are the texts of the previous four main English verse translations. In my own estimation, the result supports the claim that my translation is truer to the original than theirs.

None of the others consistently translates accurately. Some of them partly or completely ignore the metre, so creating an emotional impression that is at odds with what I am convinced the Latin poet had in mind. Others shun the rhyming formula that is one of the main attractions of the original Latin poem. Finally, some of them take far more latitude than is justified in their interpretations of the Latin version by introducing irrelevancies and flights of fancy that are not in the original.

In these instances the word 'translation' is not genuinely warranted. Instead, 'interpretation' or 'rendition' would be more accurate.

The result of this is that modern readers or hearers of the poem may not only miss entirely the exact meaning of the original words but will also be given a very false picture of which emotion the poet wanted to generate and what purpose that emotion was designed to serve.

My contention is that only a translation that, as far as possible, faithfully communicates the poet's words, thoughts and emotions and preserves the metre and rhyming system, can convey in another language an authentic version of the original.

Such an achievement imposes its own constraints. I do not think anyone can properly comprehend the strength and depth of feeling in the *Stabat Mater* without knowing something about the life and personality of the poet.

In turn, that requires some degree of knowledge of the times he lived in and the events that shaped him. That is why I have included here chapters on the Middle Ages, the ambivalent record of the Roman Catholic Church and the horrendous history of the calamitous fourteenth century and its gruesome events that may have first popularised the *Stabat Mater* some half a century after the poet's death.

With all this background information, I was able to draft a version of the poem that I hope to show is much closer to the original in language, mood and emotional effect than the previous ones. I have no doubt that some readers, especially those who understand Latin and can appreciate the power and thrust of the original poem, may find my translation somewhat less aggressive. For that reason, I have devoted some pages to an explanation of the standard requirements of translation and of the specific difficulties when the source and target languages are respectively Latin and English.

I do not want to give the impression that I am a leading historian, an expert in translating or a learned professor who has spent a lifetime researching the *Stabat Mater*. I am a retired 94-year-old Irish journalist with a handful of books and several hundreds of articles to my credit.

It is only since the idea of writing the book struck me that I have begun to do some detailed research into the background of the poem—the Catholic Church in the Middle Ages, its place in society, the role of the Popes, the development of religious orders, the ordinary people's practice of religion—and so on.

Even before I started any research, I decided to impose three constraints on myself. The first was that I would not commence translating the poem until I was thoroughly familiar with it. So I read and re-read it, reciting it to myself in order to recreate in my own mind and heart the emotions the poet felt and which he wished to produce in those who recite or sing it.

Secondly, I determined to do as much research as possible into the background facts—what were conditions like at the time the poem was thought to have been written, who was the presumed author, what might have been his motivation (I had never any doubt about it being a he) and so on.

Finally, I decided not to read the existing English translations before I had completed my own first draft version. This was to ensure that I would not be influenced by either the words or the poetic style of the earlier translators.

If the result is to throw some light on a small corner of religious poetry and, in doing so, prove that old age and physical disability are not wholly destructive of the human spirit, I will be well satisfied.

Desmond Fisher
Dublin
15 September 2014
Feast of Our Lady of Sorrows

1

A FANATIC BUT NOT A FANTASIST

Y FIRST ASSIGNMENT was to draft a plan for the book. It would require a considerable amount of preliminary research into the history of the Middle Ages, the Popes who figured in the story of the *Stabat Mater*, the 'Black Death' plague that swept through Europe and the anti-Jewish pogrom that followed it. It would also include research on the state of the Catholic Church, prosody, the peculiarities of language and the art of translating.

However, because there is a lot of disagreement and little reliable information about the early history of the *Stabat Mater*, I decided to approach the task from the point of view of the poet.

I took this in three stages. The first was to identify what sort of personal emotional feelings the poet had and was expressing in his verse. To anyone hearing or reading the original Latin the answer seemed obvious. It was a forceful desire to share in the agony of Christ's passion and death on the cross and in the corresponding sufferings of his mother.

The second stage was less obvious but even more demanding. It was his determination to share their sufferings, not just in an imaginary and symbolic fashion, but to experience them in a realistic and physical way that involved genuine self-inflicted pain. Most of the existing English translations fail to convey this sentiment.

For me the third stage was to find the cryptic key to discover the hidden significance of the poem. As one studies it, it becomes apparent that the poet was not a man to keep his feelings to himself. So the next step was to determine what reaction he intended to create in his readers and listeners. And since it turned out later that he was something of an extremist, my conclusion was that he was, in effect, challenging them to react to the Crucifixion as he himself had. He wanted them to be carried along by the same intense passion he felt, to experience the same sense of outrage as he had and to share genuinely in Christ's and Mary's sufferings.

It had taken me several months of searching the Internet to reach these conclusions. But what before, on reading or reciting the poem, had seemed to be extreme and even irrational now made perfect sense. I now felt able to follow the poet's thoughts and interpret his words uninfluenced by any extraneous considerations. I determined that, in as far as the limitations of translation permit, I would incorporate these insights into the English version of the poem I hoped eventually to produce.

This preliminary work had also resulted in producing a considerable amount of facts that were new to me about language, the conventions regarding translation, the state of the church in Europe at the time the poem was probably written and the most likely reasons the poet had for writing it.

It had also enabled me to determine, at least to my own satisfaction, which of the most likely candidates was the poem's author, why he wrote it in the way he did, what effect he wanted it to create and why he sought that outcome.

This time there was an unexpected development. As I recited the poem to myself, conscious of its mounting emotional tension, I was suddenly reminded of an Easter Week procession in Andalusia. No one who has witnessed one of these *Semana Santa* parades or *pasos*, as they are called, could forget the spectacle and the atmosphere—the menacing look of the *capriotes*, the men in thin conical hoods like Ku Klux Klan members, the white robes of the marching men, the black dresses and black veils of the women and the slow rhythmic march of the *costalores* carrying the towering floats holding statues of Jesus and Mary.

All the time drums or trumpets are beating out a slow, intense rhythm. That is what came to mind as I repeated the *Stabat Mater* to myself while sitting at my computer and looking across to the opposite wall at George Campbell's painting of the *Semana Santa* procession in Seville.

Looking at it, I suddenly remembered a scene I had witnessed on a television programme about one of these processions—a group of men walking along striking their backs with whips in time to the singing. At the time, their behaviour struck me as a bit theatrical. I could understand someone wanting to engage in self-punishment as a form of penance but why do it in public and, judging by their somewhat ostentatious behaviour, why seek to draw appreciative attention to it?

Taking a lead from this, I did some further research. And that is how I eventually found a pointer to what made the *Stabat Mater* poet wish those hearing or reading it to engage in self-punishment and to do it in such a conspicuous fashion. From that it would be only a short step to determine which of the contenders for the honour was the most likely composer of the *Stabat Mater* and an explanation of why the poem was written.

The profile of the author that emerged from my preliminary investigation was not, as the emeritus Pope Benedict XVI maintains, that of Innocent III, one of the most powerful Popes in Church history. Instead, as I will explain in a later chapter, the facts indicate compellingly that the *Stabat Mater* was the work of the other main contender, a fanatical Franciscan friar who renounced his wealthy lifestyle after his wife's tragic death and became an itinerant rhymester.

So when I started on the actual translation I hoped to be familiar enough with his history to feel able to follow his thoughts and interpret his words uninfluenced by any extraneous considerations.

My main conclusion is that the original Latin *Stabat Mater* is a more functional and down to earth hymn than some of the earlier translators would lead one to believe. It certainly is not the sentimental lyric or the frenzied jabbering that some of them express. Rather it is the work of someone who is certainly a fanatic but not a fantasist, a religious zealot with a more pragmatic and less high-minded objective in mind than was my earlier reaction.

Neither is the poet of the *Stabat Mater* in the same league as his contemporary Dante (he was born thirty-two years before Dante and died fifteen years before him) with a highly developed theological framework on which to build something as sublime as the *Divine Comedy*. Nor is the *Stabat Mater* in the same class as the Evangelist Luke's inspiring *Magnificat*, Mary's soaring hymn of praise to God for choosing her as the mother of his son.

The *Stabat Mater's* versifier is more of a journeyman poet producing a hymn for a specific purpose and using the story of the Crucifixion as its kernel. The fact that it turned out to be a highly regarded and world famous Marian hymn was a bonus. If, as some historians claim, the author was one of the leading poets in the Italy of the Middle Ages, that could validate my verdict that the *Stabat Mater* rates among the greatest works in prosody.

Whoever the poet was—and I will later explain the reasons for my own preference—I believe his aim was, by means of rhythm, rhyme and choice of words, to paint a harrowing picture of the first Good Friday on Calvary. This would, he hoped, enkindle in his listeners, readers and singers an intense remorse and generate in them a near-hypnotic impulse to practise intense self-punishment.

Why he should want to do that is one of the questions that this book sets out to answer.

2

THE FIRST GOOD FRIDAY

HE FIRST NECESSITY for a translator of the *Stabat Mater* is to determine, as far as this is possible, what had motivated the poet to write the poem in the first place. What were his thoughts as he imagined himself pushing his way through the crowd of jeering onlookers on the hill of Calvary on that first Good Friday? Could he see or hear Jesus as he hung on his cross, moaning and making some almost incoherent remarks while his weeping mother was huddled to one side being comforted by her friends?

So I put myself in the poet's hands or, to put it more colloquially, into his boots. His eyes are now my eyes and I will see what he sees and try to feel what he feels.

We start off, as the poet himself would say, *in medias res*. We are now standing on the hill just outside the old wall of Jerusalem where convicted criminals are crucified by the Roman occupiers of Palestine. A rock shaped like a bald human head gives part of the hill its Hebrew name of Golgotha, the place of the skull.

On the hill today are three crosses where three Jewish men have been hanging since early morning. It is now mid-afternoon and the Roman soldiers are getting a bit nervy. They are under pressure to get the men down off their crosses. The Jewish custom is that day ends at dusk and therefore a dead person must be buried before nightfall.

Today the soldiers are under more pressure than normal. Tomorrow is the Shabbat of Pesach, the

Passover Sabbath, celebrating the Exodus; the day
Moses freed the Jews from their slavery in Egypt.

Two of the crucified men were robbers, so their
corpses will be disposed of quickly in the paupers' pit.
But there is some problem over a grave for the man on
the middle cross—they call him Jesus of Nazareth. He
is some sort of a religious revolutionary and he caused
a bit of trouble the other day when he knocked over
all the merchants' stalls in the Temple courtyard and
chased them out.

The problem seems to be that he is a Galilean and the
family has no grave in this part of Palestine. Those two
men over there say they are making the necessary
arrangements. The tall man is Joseph of Arimathea. He
has hewn himself a grave into the side of this hill and he
has offered it for Jesus, as well as the linen for a shroud.
The smaller man is Nicodemus, who seems to be a
believer in Jesus. You can see he has the myrrh and aloes
in his hands for rubbing on Jesus' body. First, they will
have to get permission from Pontius Pilate, the Roman
Governor, to bury Jesus here.

But that should be easy enough. Even though they
are both members of the Sanhedrin, those two men did
not look too happy last night about the way Jesus was
being treated. So Pilate will be glad to oblige them. He
would like to get his own back on the Sanhedrin for
forcing him to condemn Jesus to death against his own
judgment. But first he needs confirmation that Jesus is
dead. The soldiers break his legs like they did with the
others to hurry things up. That's probably why the
centurion has just now stuck his spear into Jesus' side
to make sure.

Indeed, he already looked half-dead this morning
when they forced him to carry his cross all the way up

here. He was in a very bad way and looked awful. Only for that Simon of Cyrene fellow they forced to help him, he would surely have died on the road. He must have had a really terrible time since they arrested him last night over there to the East on the Mount of Olives. Strange! Only a week ago they were throwing palm branches under his feet and calling him the Messiah. Last night they were dragging him over and back across the city looking for someone to condemn him to death.

They took him first to the house of Annas, across the wall there in the Upper City. Annas has no powers of jurisdiction so he sent Jesus over to his son-in-law, Caiphas, who is this year's High Priest. Caiphas has had it in for Jesus after the carry-on at the Temple. He immediately put Jesus on trial before the Sanhedrin and asked him was he really claiming to be the son of God.

Then when Jesus answered something like 'You've said it', he was charged with blasphemy and, despite a bit of opposition, Caiphas persuaded the Sanhedrin to impose the death penalty. Of course, that's really *ultra vires* for the Sanhedrin, so first thing this morning they took Jesus to Pilate to get their verdict ratified.

Pilate is deep enough in Rome's bad books at present without risking another complication. Everyone knows Tiberias wants no trouble in his Empire and that he will have no hesitation in getting rid of Pilate permanently if the Jews are not kept in line. Anyway, they say Pilate's wife had a dream about Jesus and told her husband to have nothing to do with him because he was an upright man.

So when he heard Jesus was from Galilee and that Herod Antipas, the Tetrarch of that part of Palestine, was in Jerusalem for the Passover ceremonies, he sent

Jesus to him to deal with. But Herod is too long in the tooth to be caught up in tricky political matters like that. He just thanked Pilate for his courtesy and sent Jesus back to him.

By then, the High Priests and the Sanhedrin were getting really irritated with all the fruitless comings and goings because it was beginning to annoy the people. They had paid good money to one of his disciples to tip them off about his movements and he had led Jesus into their hands. Then they had whipped up a mob to create trouble and briefed witnesses to make false allegations against Jesus that would convince the Romans he was a danger. They wanted to get things over before the Sabbath.

It was too late to do any more last night. So, first thing this morning, they gathered up the mob and landed back at Pilate's palace demanding action. Overnight they had come up with a few new charges against Jesus that they were confident would force Pilate's hand. They told him that Jesus was claiming to be the son of God and king of the Jews and was saying that they should pay no more taxes to Rome.

That was something Pilate could not ignore. Previous Roman emperors had called themselves 'son of the God' so there could be trouble in someone else posing as Son of God. Then, to be called 'King of the Jews' is a real challenge to Rome. On top of all that, to advocate the withholding of tax is a capital offence in the empire. Pilate just had to act.

First, he had Jesus mercilessly scourged and when the soldiers crowned him with thorns he brought Jesus out, all covered in blood, to show him to the mob, hoping that would satisfy their blood lust. But the crowd was having none of it. They turned very nasty and Pilate feared a riot. He even offered to let them choose between releasing Jesus or that criminal Barabbas for the usual Passover amnesty. They chose Barabbas.

And then he really let himself down. He, the Governor of Jerusalem, who has a record of treating Jews like dirt, actually asked them what he should do now with Jesus. You could hear them as far away as Bethany shouting out 'Crucify him, crucify him.'

There was something really pathetic about what Pilate did next. Maybe he was trying to pacify his wife. He called for a basin of water and a towel to be brought out. There and then, he very ostentatiously washed his hands, calling on the mob to notice he was declaring himself innocent of the blood of what he called in his own words 'this just man.'

If he thought that would impress the mob he was badly mistaken. It seemed to enrage them all the more. They shouted out: 'Let his blood be on us and on our children.' Pilate looked really apprehensive as if he feared they would actually break into his palace and kill him on the spot. So he released Jesus to be crucified. And in very quick time a centurion and a cohort of soldiers were ordered to make him take up a cross and carry it up the steep road here to Calvary.

We saw for ourselves what happened after that. We heard the thud the mallets made as they hammered the spikes into Jesus' hands and feet. They tied a notice on his head in Hebrew, Greek and Latin saying 'Jesus of Nazareth King of the Jews'.

This morning we saw the old blood on his head where the crown of thorns had been pressed down last night and the fresh blood on his side as the spear was driven home a minute ago. We heard the crowd jeering Jesus, saying he claimed he could save others, so why didn't he save himself. We heard him saying he was thirsty and they rubbed a cloth dipped in sour wine on his face but he turned his head away. Then he whispered something to one of the robbers hanging beside him that this day he would be in Paradise. And you might have heard him just now saying what sounded like 'It's all over.'

Indeed it does look like that. The men on the crosses seem to be very near death if they are not already dead. A short while ago we saw the skies suddenly darkening over. Then, just a minute ago, we heard that small earthquake. Now they're saying the tombs in the cemetery further up the hill have burst open and that the veil of the Temple on the far side of the city has split down the middle.

You can see his mother is pushing her way through the crowds that are beginning to go back into the city. All these long hours, she and a few other women have been following what has been happening since last night when Jesus was arrested. They have been standing over there comforting her all day. Those other Galilean men that he called his disciples fled last night because they were understandably afraid for their own lives.

The soldiers are now lining up to leave. They did not cut up Jesus' robe between them as they normally do with clothes if they are worth keeping. Usually, of course, they are just rags. Perhaps they think their centurion might have been right when they heard him say: 'Truly he was the son of God.' Maybe the robe could be sold to a souvenir hunter for a few *denarii*. Better toss for it before taking it back to barracks.

Mary, Jesus' mother, and the other women are standing as close as they can get to the cross as Joseph and Nicodemus take his body down. She is looking distraught, as well she might. It must have been very hard for her, especially near the end, to hear her son crying out in agony to someone he called his god. He was asking why he had been abandoned. Then he said it was all over and now, as you can see, he is dead.

Mary must be wondering about the people who were jeering her son on the cross. Had they forgotten that the man they were sneering at was the same man who had cured their sick, raised people from the dead and fed multitudes with a few small pieces of bread and a few fish? The stupidity of all that had happened, the insensitivity, the total unreasonableness of it all must be making her almost despair, doubting the goodness of God and questioning what her life and the life of her son had all been about.

Who could not sympathise with her in her torment of mind? Who could look at her and not also shed tears like her? As darkness begins to fall and the crowds move down through the gate and into the city, memories of what she was told in the past must be coming back to her. Was the angel fooling her when he told her the Holy Spirit would come upon her and the power of the Highest would overshadow her so that her child would be called the Son of God?

Or was she thinking of what the old man Simeon said to her that morning long ago when she took her baby son to the Temple to be circumcised? No-one could forget that warning: 'Behold, this child is appointed for the fall and rising of many in Israel, and for a sign that is opposed, and a sword will pierce through your own soul also, so that thoughts from many hearts may be revealed.' (Luke 2: 34–35)

And where are the men he had called on to follow him? One of them had betrayed him to the authorities and the rest must have fled back to Galilee except for the gentle one, John, whom he named as her son.

Had she heard aright when he seemed to be calling on his heavenly Father not to abandon him? Had … Had … Had … ? The questions keep swirling round her troubled head as she and her little band of women companions, really the most loyal of her son's followers, crowd round the men now placing his body in the cave.

3

THE POET'S VERSION

S THE ROMAN soldiers and the last Jewish spectators leave Calvary, the stage is left to the poet of the *Stabat Mater* to compose his poem. His main characters are Christ and his mother, both of whom play only passive roles, with himself in the lead as a representative of the human race.

His mental picture of Calvary is stark. Jesus is still hanging on his cross, his dead body dangling loosely forward and his head twisted sideways to the right. Mary stands on his left side, looking downwards and with her hands joined. She is crying pitifully as the questions still swirl round her head and the sword still pierces her heart.

We have no way of knowing how much Mary understands God's purpose in condemning his son and hers to such a fate. Can she comprehend why he had to suffer such pain, such degradation and such rejection by the people he had come to save?

Had she felt the urge to push her way through the jeering crowd to reach up and clasp her son's feet and try to lift him down? She had seen his body still bloody and scarred from the scourging, his forehead marked where the thorns had pierced, his feet and hands bleeding, his face screwed up in agony. The memories of that awful day on Calvary will never leave her.

At first, the poet portrays himself as an uncommitted but sympathetic observer. He describes Mary's woeful state as she weeps for her dead son. Sad, dejected, tearful, doleful—the sonorous adjectives stream out as he takes in the enormity of the outrage that has just taken place. That is the theme of the first four stanzas of the poem.

Then he realises that this is not just a spectator event that does not involve him personally. What human being, seeing the dead Christ's mother so afflicted, could not but weep with her? Who would not want to share her suffering? She had seen her son scourged and in torment as he was punished for the sins of the very creatures his divine father had created. She had watched him dying in desolation and apparently abandoned as he gave up his spirit. This is the theme of the next four stanzas.

Evidently overwhelmed by the tragedy of the event, the poet now wants to play an active role in the tragedy that is Calvary. He turns to address Mary directly. In the next nine stanzas of mounting emotion, he implores, almost demands, of her that she allow him to grieve with her, to make his heart burn with love for Jesus, to let him feel the nails being driven though his own hands and feet.

Working himself up into a passion, he asks Mary not to be bitter with him but to let him 'carry Christ's death', to be a partner in his passion, to share the scourges and to become immersed—the poet's word is 'intoxicated'—in the blood from his side. It is these stanzas particularly that give the hymn its powerful sweep and overwhelming emotional force.

In the last three of the poem's twenty stanzas the scene and the mood change. We are no longer on Calvary offering our consolation to a desolate mother watching her son dying on the cross. Mary is now crowned in glory as Queen of Heaven. It is Judgment

Day at the end of the world and we humans are being divided into the saved and the damned. Addressing Mary as the Virgin, the poet pleads with her to defend him against being burned.

In the final two stanzas the poet speaks directly to Christ. This is not the shattered figure on the cross but now the risen Christ sitting at the right hand of God in heaven. First, the poet asks him to let his mother ensure he gets the palm of victory. Finally, he asks Jesus directly to make certain the poet's soul is given the glory of Paradise.

Even this comparatively bland English prose description conveys some impression of force, urgency and audacity. In Latin, swathed in the pounding rhythm of the metre, the text studded with long and resounding words and declaiming a list of requests that sound more like commands, the effect is astounding. How the Rev Matthew Britt, OSB, as quoted in the Catholic Culture website, could refer in 1880 to the *Stabat Mater* as 'the tenderest and most touching hymn of the Middle Ages' is difficult to understand.

What the poet wants to achieve is now clear. His intention is to recreate Calvary so vividly that it becomes for him a present reality. He speaks directly to Mary and Jesus, demanding to share their sufferings personally. So direct is his language and so authentic his emotion that, for a while, the reader might feel slightly uncomfortable as if being caught eavesdropping on a private occasion.

By the poem's end, however, readers or listeners are no longer mere onlookers of a routine Roman execution in an occupied province. Drawn subconsciously into the proceedings by the momentum of the words, the vibrant metre and the sonorous rhymes, they react instinctively.

The first instinct is one of shock and sorrow as the story of Calvary is retold and its outrage recalled to mind. This is followed by a feeling of anger and shame at the realisation that this is a crime the human race has committed against the Saviour who had come to redeem it. Finally, the mood created by the poem is a desire to share the sufferings of Mary and her son, if not through actual self-punishment, then at least in spirit.

This is an interpretation of the *Stabat Mater* that is different in tone and in substance from the rather saccharine depictions of Christ's mother in some of the translations. The Virgin of the poem weeps in her agony and deserves to be comforted but she is also strong enough to accept her destiny and, as the poet sees her, is able to accomplish things beyond human competence.

The poet also treats those who read or sing his verse as active participants with him in humankind's spiritual journey. As will become clearer later on, his poem is written for a specific reason. He is one of those many people, both cleric and lay, in the Middle Ages who believe that the world is coming to an end. Meanwhile, life has a serious purpose and a true believer has a duty to make up for the failings of others.

The poet's conviction is that this responsibility to atone for personal and communal sins and to ward off the eternal punishment they merit can be fulfilled by suffering, especially self-administered punishment, here on earth. For him, the Crucifixion is the paramount example of such atonement. It is the individual's obligation to emulate it.

This is the *leitmotif* of the *Stabat Mater* and its significance is missed if that interpretation is lost in sentimentalism. The most rewarding way of understanding the role of the Virgin Mary at Calvary is not simply as a helpless mother weeping over her dying son, but as an advocate for the whole human race. Her grief is not only for herself but also for those who had insulted their Creator and executed His and her son and who would continue to do so to the end of time. The sword that pierced her heart on Calvary was the recognition that the God/man she had borne had been rejected by the people he loved and had come to save.

So much can be learned from just reading, reciting and reflecting on the Latin text that encapsulates the emotional feelings the poet experiences and is impelled to express. But the poem's magnetism does not end there. It also induces the reader or listener to observe the same scenes in the same way as the poet did, to share his horror and incomprehension, to react in the same way and to share a similar spiritual experience.

To produce these reactions he uses a poet's tools— metre, rhyme and words. My challenge as his translator is to use the same tools in an attempt to create the same reactions in a language that is very different from his. It will be interesting to discover if it can be done.

4

THE FLAGELLANTI

PUNISHMENT, WHETHER INFLICTED by another or self-administered, is a central part of the *Stabat Mater* story. The practice of whipping or scourging, both as a punishment and as a self-motivated penance, goes back a very long way.

Early hermits and anchorites practised it on themselves in the Egyptian desert. The Romans used it on rebellious slaves and insubordinate soldiers; the British used it on mutinous sailors and lawbreakers in their penal colonies; the southern American cotton planters used it on their African slaves. It is still used in several former British territories in South-East Asia and Africa.

As far as Christianity is concerned, the punishment goes back to the beginning when Pilate ordered Jesus to be scourged, a routine practice before a Roman crucifixion. What we call the Scourging at the Pillar is known in the Latin liturgy as *Flagellatio*, which translates as 'scourging' or 'whipping.'

In the Middle Ages, self-administered or even compulsory flagellation was adopted by some of the religious orders as a way of showing sorrow for their own sins and to appease God for the sins or failings of others.

The first of these monasteries, Subiaco, in the province of Rome, was founded in 509 AD by St Benedict. For the next seven hundred years, new Orders appeared with monasteries being established all over Europe.

Most of the earliest monasteries followed the Benedictine rule but in the eleventh century many other orders were established — the Cistercians (1058), Franciscans (1029), Carmelites (1206), Dominicans (1215), Servites (1223) and the Augustinians (1244) — with a less Spartan discipline.

Lay people were also caught up in a fervour to escape a world they saw as corrupt and dangerous. They sought to save themselves from the wrath of a God who seemed to be punishing the planet with plagues, crop failures, wars and other catastrophes that they regarded as signs of his wrath.

By the tenth century many such lay groups or 'sodalities', as they came to be called, were formed in central Italy. Some of them were started by wealthy upper class men dissatisfied with their purposeless existence. Wanting to live a Christian life, but not as celibate clerics, they set out to do good in their own way. Some of the more austere of them voluntarily abandoned their homes, gave away their assets and lived frugally.

Their main way of doing good was to look after the poor, the sick and the homeless and to bury the dead. They also provided dowries for poor young women and ransoms for soldiers taken captive in wars between Italy's rival city-states or in the Crusades.

In the twelfth and thirteenth centuries, when parts of Italy were struck by famine, pestilence or drought, these sodalities evolved into two different groups. One that included the *Laudesi* (praisers) and *Bianchi* (whites) paraded round the cities and the surrounding area singing songs glorifying God and appealing to him for mercy.

Later, another group took personal mortification of the flesh as a way to salvation. These bands had names like the *Battuti* (Beaters) describing how they acted or were dressed. Using scourges of cord tipped with broken glass or pieces of sharp metal, marching penitents lashed themselves in time with the chanting, often till their clothes and backs were covered in blood. In this way they believed their self-inflicted punishment would atone for their own sins and the sins of the world that merited the anger of a vengeful God.

In 1259, following one of the frequent plagues, one such group in the Umbrian city of Perugia became very influential. It appointed leaders who, twice a day, administered punishment to penitents lying bare-footed and stripped to the waist in a circle in the church or in the main square.

The penitents confessed their sins in a bizarre way. Murderers lay on their backs, adulterers face down, perjurers on their sides holding up three fingers. After a while, they were ordered to stand and the lay team leaders scourged them before ordering them to continue scourging themselves. Penitents had to follow this procedure for the thirty-three and a half days the band walked from place to place in memory of Christ's years of life.

In three years, the *Flagellanti* movement had spread to France, Austria, Germany, Poland and Sweden. By now it was causing concern in the Vatican. Its leaders were bypassing the churches and the priests and seemed to be turning into something approaching a do-it-yourself religion. They claimed that priests were not needed to administer the sacraments since they themselves could absolve their followers from sin and cast out evil spirits. This was too much for Rome.

Accusing the movement of heresy, the Pope banned it
in 1261 and excommunicated its leaders.

At first, the leaders tried to outface the Pope and
pledged to keep going for at least thirty-three years or
even to found a rival church. But their posturing was
unsuccessful and the movement collapsed.

Or so it seemed. But eighty-five years later, it was
to be reborn in a far more formidable shape. In 1346,
humankind was struck by one of the greatest catastrophes ever known. As millions died and those still alive
believed the world was coming to an end, the flagellant
movement was resurrected to become stronger than
ever.

It was in this eighty-five-year interval between the
Pope's original ban and the outbreak of the plague
that, as nearly as I can ascertain, the *Stabat Mater* was
written and later became one of the most popular items
in the flagellants' repertoire.

Undoubtedly its appeal to the marching bands was
because of the way it projects the insistent rhythm of
its metre and reflects the heavyweight pounding of the
three- and four-syllable Latin words that give it a
dignity and a menacing authority.

These qualities help to create the hypnotic effect that
encourages the flagellants to keep marching, all the
while singing and scourging themselves, until they
bleed. As they trudge along the dusty roads, the
convention is that immediately the group is ordered
to stop, everyone falls to the ground on the spot, no
matter how hard or dirty the ground beneath is.

In my translation of the poem I have tried to convey
this sense of urgency and insistency as accurately as
the limitations of translation permit.

5

WHO WROTE THE POEM?

 NE OF MY earliest objectives was to determine, at least to my own satisfaction, which of the seven listed contenders was the most likely to have been the composer of the *Stabat Mater* poem. However, my research found no agreement on the question.

Even such an authoritative source as the US *Catholic Encyclopaedia* is not sure about the matter. It opts somewhat tentatively for Pope Innocent III (d. 1216) as the author though it lists as other challengers St Gregory the Great (d. 604), St Bernard of Clairvaux (d. 1153), St Bonaventure (d. 1274), Jacopone da Todi (d. 1306), Pope John XXII (d. 1334) and Pope Gregory XI (d. 1378). Most other sources, however, shorten the list to the two they regard as the likeliest—Innocent III and Jacopone da Todi.

After examining the biographies of all seven probable authors, I found myself in agreement with majority opinion in cutting the short list down to these two.

My judgment call was based on the belief that, as I mentioned before, the poem would not have been written at any time earlier than the middle of the thirteenth century or the first half of the fourteenth. That was when the flagellant movement was relatively inactive and the Franciscans were promoting devotion to the Virgin Mary. For me, that ruled out St Gregory the Great and St Bernard, who had died in the seventh and twelfth centuries respectively.

Of the others, St Bonaventure comes into the right time frame and has many of the qualities one might reasonably associate with the author of the *Stabat Mater*. Known as the 'Seraphic Doctor', he was a well-known theologian, a friend and near intellectual equal of St Thomas Aquinas and was reported to have experienced ecstasies.

At the age of 36, he was elected Minister General of the Franciscan Friars Minor at a time when the order was split between two staunchly opposed factions. One, called the *Spirituales*, wanted to live apart, faithfully observing the original rule of St Francis which decreed the strictest poverty, solitary meditation and self-administered physical punishment. The other faction of *Relaxati* or *Conventuales* favoured a less rigid regime that would permit them to live as a community and work in the outside world serving the poor and the sick.

Bonaventure's sympathies probably lay with the stricter group but his priority had to be to hold the conflicting factions together. So, even if he were himself to be a self-chastiser, he was unlikely to have been a populist promoter of the flagellants as the poet of the *Stabat Mater* seems to have been. That ruled him out for me.

Pope John XXII is an interesting choice and a legitimate contender inasmuch as he was a recognised composer of hymns. Two of his poems that have come down to us are known in English as 'Soul of Christ, sanctify me' and 'Soul of my Saviour, sanctify my breast'. However, his extravagant lifestyle did not conform with his poetic emotions. The second of the seven Avignon Popes, he was constantly involved in controversy with clerical and secular opponents.

For most of his reign of eighteen years he taught that those who died in the faith did not see the presence of God until the Last Judgment, withdrawing this assertion only shortly before his death.

He also intervened very forcibly to end the split in the Franciscan order, issuing a bull condemning those so-called *Fraticelli* Franciscans who preached extreme forms of poverty and exaggerated discipline. His argument was that obedience was more important than poverty and that there was nothing in scripture to prevent clerics from owning property.

John XXII died in 1334,[1] some fourteen years before the Great Plague struck Europe and the flagellants became active again after a long period of inactivity. His rough handling of the more austere wing of the Franciscans persuaded me that he was not the writer of the punishment-inviting *Stabat Mater*.

Pope Gregory XI was born c. 1330 and so was about eighteen years of age when the plague arrived in Europe and forty-eight when the first wave abated. So from the age point of view he could qualify for inclusion in the list. He was forty when he was elected Pope[2] and was the last of the seven Popes who based themselves in Avignon, returning the papacy to Rome in 1377 after receiving a scathing reproach from St Catherine of Siena.[3]

His death less than a year later triggered the so-called Western Schism when three men were simultaneously claiming the papacy in succession to him. It was a time when the greater schism that would become known as the Protestant Reformation was incubating in Germany and England and not a time when Popes would be engaged in writing poetry. I ruled him out also.

Of the named candidates, that left only the two front-runners, Pope Innocent III and Jacopone da Todi. Expert opinion has been divided between them for a long time without any likelihood that a definitive answer will ever be found.

Among those who have opted for Pope Innocent is Emeritus Pope Benedict XVI. This is not altogether surprising since existing Popes often honour their predecessors.

Certainly, Innocent III was the outstanding Pope of the Middle Ages and one of the most influential Popes in history. He came from the powerful dei Conti family whose various branches contributed nine Popes to the Church, including Boniface VIII, who would play a major role in Jacopone da Todi's life story.

In January 1198, on the very day his predecessor Celestine III died and when he himself was only thirty-seven, he was unanimously elected Pope.[4] In his first year in office, Innocent initiated a crusade against the Albigensian heresy in the South of France, resulting in the death of twenty thousand Cathars. He also summoned the Fourth Crusade to liberate Jerusalem from the Moslems, an undertaking that ended in the destruction of Constantinople in 1204.[5]

He was also a great religious reformer and called the Fourth Lateran Council to issue a series of seventy decrees to clean up corruption and laxity in the Church. He has several theological tracts to his credit and is known to have written poetry in his earlier years. But, in my view, he is very unlikely to have had time to compose poems during his papacy, especially one so humane and so theologically dubious as the *Stabat Mater*. He died in 1216,[6] one hundred and seventy two years before the Genoa reference.[7] Even though word of mouth was the customary means of communication at that time, that seems a long period for a Pope's composition to become known.

Having ruled out him and the others, my own preference—and up to recently accepted as the most likely claimant—is Jacopone da Todi. He is the only layperson in the list of candidates and his background is not so prestigious as those of his titled rivals. What makes him my favourite is that he is a man who has suffered greatly and whose emotions are similar to those expressed in the poem. In fact, some of his poems — and he turned out to be one of the best-known of the thirteenth century Italian poets — were almost identical in theme and in feeling to those in the *Stabat Mater.*

The more I discovered about his life, the more he fitted the image of the poem's creator that I had shaped in my mind. Reciting the poem to myself and trying to put myself in the poet's place, I visualized a man driven by some deep emotion and needing some form of action to release the tension within him. The man I saw had a chip on his shoulder, a one-track mind and a burning wish to do whatever it took to atone for past failings and to convince others to follow his example.

Such a man would not have been a philosopher or a theologian lost in the higher strata of speculation nor a Pope planning crusades and embroiled in diplomatic manoeuvres.

He was a man like the rest of us but with a lot of grievances and a gift for writing poetry in which to express them. Both the Latin *Stabat Mater* about the torture Christ and Mary experienced at Calvary and the Umbrian poems about the mental tortures he himself was enduring decidedly point the finger at Jacopone. I would not be satisfied until I knew more about him.

Notes

1 J. J. Norwich, *The Popes* (London: Vintage Books, 2012) p. 204.
2 *Ibid.*, pp. 216–222.
3 *Ibid.*, p. 217.
4 *Ibid.*, p. 165.
5 *Ibid.*, p. 166.
6 *Ibid.*, p. 171.
7 See Roman Catholic Saints, www.roman-catholic-saints.com/
   blessed-jacopone-of-todi.html. See also p. 43 below.

6

SILLY JAMES FROM TODI

ISTORY KNOWS HIM as Jacopone da Todi. His given name was Jacopo dei Benedetti. He was the scion of a noble family from Todi, a small hill town in Umbria, in the centre of Italy.

The date of his birth is uncertain but was probably between 1228 and 1236, thirteen years or more after Innocent's death. He studied law in Bologna and for some years was one of Todi's leading lawyers, with a nobly-born and beautiful wife, Vanna di Guidone, daughter of the Count of the nearby town of Collemedio.

One day in 1268—this date is also uncertain— Donna Vanna had, at her husband's urging, dressed in her best attire and gone into town to attend a fashionable social function in the Piazza del Popolo, the main square of Todi. With the town's other upper class ladies, she was standing on an elevated platform when the whole structure collapsed.

Crushed in the wreckage, she was the only person fatally wounded. Under her fashionable clothes, she was found to have been wearing a hairshirt. Her shocked husband took this as her way of atoning for his greed, vanity and extravagant lifestyle.

Utterly devastated by her death and feeling ashamed by her secret self-mortification, Jacopone threw up his job, abandoned his house and family name, disposed of all his assets and gave the money to the poor.

Aged in his forties, he turned his back on a world he now saw as evil and corrupt and took to wandering the hilly Umbrian roads, dressed in an old *bizocone*, the hairy shirt of Franciscan lay tertiaries, and living off what grew on the hedges or what food the peasants gave him.

He was so wretched-looking that the local young-sters, whether out of contempt or friendly compassion, gave him the nickname of Jacopone, which variously translates as 'Big Jim' or 'Silly Jim'. The custom of the time was not to use surnames but, rather, to add to the Christian name the name of the birthplace. So we get Italian names such as Leonardo da Vinci, a town in Tuscany. Hence Jacopone da Todi.

So radical was his rejection of his past life and so extreme his fear of death and eternal punishment that his behaviour convinced his family and former friends that he was mad.

On one occasion he went to a wedding party in his brother's house, naked, smeared in honey and covered in feathers. On another he is said to have agreed to help a friend by carrying to the man's home two chickens he had bought in the market. When the chickens could not be found, Jacopone led the man to the cemetery where he had buried them in the man's family's plot which he said was his real home.

In 1278, after some ten years of wandering around Umbria's hill towns and when he was in his fifties, he applied to join the Franciscan Order in their house in Todi. The friars were understandably somewhat dubious about his suitability. Whichever of the monks opened the door is supposed to have said, half jokingly and half dismissively: 'If you wish to live with us, you must become a donkey, so that as a donkey you may dwell among the donkeys.'

If the jest was intended to repel a potential nuisance, it misfired. Soon after, Jacopone came back on all fours, stark naked and wearing only a saddle. The friars relented and took him in. However, he refused to be considered for the priesthood and entered the St Fortunato friary as a lay brother.

At this time, the last quarter of the thirteenth century, the Franciscans had spread widely and were the most dynamic of all the religious orders, outclassing the longer-established Benedictines and taking over many of their foundations.

But not too long after its foundation in 1209, the brotherhood had divided into two factions. An extremist branch, who were variously called the *Spirituali* (Devout), *Zelanti* (Zealots), or *Disciplinati* (Disciplinarians) wanted to continue living according to the Primitive Rule that Francis himself had devised and followed. This required the friars to practise absolute poverty and self-punishment of all kinds and to indulge in what today would be regarded as a morbid preoccupation with death.

Jacopone became a fervent supporter of this group. They sought but were refused permission to live in separate accommodation from the majority group of more moderate *Conventuales* who believed that a preoccupation with self-effacement obstructed their great gifts of evangelisation that were proving so effective.

As the thirteenth century came to an end, Italy itself was split into two rival camps, with Popes and Holy Roman Emperors at war with each other, sometimes literally, for supremacy. They were backed respectively by Guelphs, consisting of wealthy merchant families siding with the Pope, and Ghibellines, who

were mainly prosperous rural landowners and supporters of the Holy Roman Emperor. Their rivalry
poisoned Italy for four centuries, setting city against
city and involving the Pope, the Emperor and many
of Europe's other rulers in constant strife.

The antagonism was replicated in the Roman Curia
which was often split along Guelph/Ghibelline lines.
So when in April 1292, the Franciscan Pope Nicholas
IV died, the twelve Cardinals in the conclave were
deadlocked and remained stubbornly so for two years
and three months without electing a new Pope.

However, in July 1294, their sick old Dean, Cardinal
Latino Malabranca, found a dramatic way of ending
the impasse. Warning them of God's displeasure at
their obstinacy, he called out: 'In the name of the
Father, the Son and the Holy Ghost, I elect brother
Pietro da Morrone.'

Pietro was a seventy-nine-year-old Benedictine
hermit who lived in 1239 AD in a cavern on the
mountain of Morrone (hence his name) before moving
to an even remoter location on the 9170 ft high Monte
Amaro in the Abruzzo region of central Italy. Following the example of John the Baptist, he wore sackcloth
and chains, observed four different Lents every year
and, day or night, spent many hours in prayer and
penitential exercises.

His fame was so great and his holiness so acclaimed
that the Curia Cardinals unanimously agreed with
their Dean. Accompanied by the kings of Naples and
Hungary and a crowd of people said to number many
thousands, they climbed the mountain to invite him
to become Pope. It took days of persuasion and coer-
cion before the reluctant recluse gave in and was
unanimously elected as Pope Celestine V.

He was no sooner in office than a deputation from the radical wing of the Franciscans, including Jacopone da Todi, sought his intervention in their cause. A zealot himself, the new Pope agreed and approved the foundation of a kindred but separate order called the Poor Hermits of Pope Celestine.

This satisfied neither faction. In one of his more sombre *laude,* Jacopone predicted that the new Pope's acceptance of the papal office had put a yoke around his neck that would cause his damnation.

It was not long before his prediction was proved correct. Pope Celestine turned out to be an incompetent administrator. He made decisions that were arbitrary and sometimes even contradictory, such as appointing two or three applicants to the same office. The great wave of hope that the new Pope's election had stirred up throughout the Christian world was soon stifled.

Perhaps deliberately, in order to precipitate his own removal, he delivered so many questionable rulings in five months that a cabal of Cardinals began to seek ways of getting rid of him.

However, he anticipated them. After only 161 days in office, he issued an edict allowing a Pope to abdicate. A week later, describing the papacy as intolerable, he suddenly resigned—something only he and one earlier Pope has ever done until Benedict XVI surprised the world in February 2013. Among the reasons he gave were the desire for humility, his own ignorance, the perversity of the people and his longing for the tranquillity of his former life.

With that he gladly escaped back to his mountain hermitage. He was not to know that his contentment would be of so short a duration as it subsequently turned out to be.

7

PAPAL DISAPPROVAL

 n CHRISTMAS EVE 1294, eleven days after Pope
Celestine's abdication, the Cardinals elected
his successor. He was Cardinal Benedetto
Gaetani, who, as Boniface VIII, was even more remarkable a Pontiff than his extraordinary predecessor and
one of the most astounding of the 266 officially recognised Popes in Church history.[1]

Fearing that Celestine's supporters would plot
against him, his first action was to order his predecessor to be imprisoned. Celestine heard of the decree and
hid out in the mountains for several months before
attempting to escape to Greece. His boat was driven
back by a tempest and he was captured and incarcer-
ated in a basement cell, nine feet long and three feet
wide, in the Papal castle of Fumone. The air was so
putrid that he died the following year, 1296, at the age
of eighty-one.

Both Jacopone da Todi and Dante had criticised
him, the former for accepting the papacy in the first
place, the latter for resigning it and thus making way
for Boniface to succeed him. Dante, who was his
political opponent, consigned him to Hell for what in
his *Inferno* he called 'the great refusal'. However, in
1313, only seventeen years after his death, Clement V,
the first of the Avignon Popes, canonised him.

Three days after his enthronement, the new Pope,
in what may have been intended as a warning to his
opponents, rescinded all of his predecessor's decrees

except the one that recognised a Pope's right to resign, thus protecting his own election. Those he revoked included the one permitting Jacopone da Todi and his fellow Franciscan extremists to split away from their more moderate confrères.

Pope Boniface then set out to impress on the world that the Pope was superior to everyone else, including the most powerful of kings. Claiming that he wanted to unite Europe in a Crusade against the Moslems, he intervened in quarrels in Sicily, Venice, Genoa, Florence, Denmark, Hungary, Poland, Germany, Scotland, England and particularly in France. When papal troops were too few to impose his orders, he supplemented them by issuing papal condemnations, warnings, penalties, fines, and interdictions as well as threats of and actual excommunications.

In 1297, Boniface clashed with two of his own Cardinals, members of the powerful Colonna family, which for merely political reasons had sided with Jacopone and the Franciscan Spirituals. These two Cardinals, with the support of some other leading Italian families with an eye on the papacy, drew up a manifesto calling for the abdication of Celestine V to be annulled and Boniface's election declared invalid. Among the leading clerics and nobles officially witnessing the manifesto was the ex-lawyer Jacopone da Todi under his official name of Frater Jacobus de Tuderto.

Boniface lost no time in answering the challenge. All the signatories to the manifesto, including the two Colonna Cardinals and Jacopone, were excommunicated. Meantime, rival families had entered the fray and the quarrel developed into a full-scale war between the two sides.

The Pope had cunningly appointed one of the younger Colonnas to lead the papal army which won the day against his own family. Except for its Cathedral, the city of Palestrina, the family's ancestral home, was razed to the ground, its six thousand citizens slaughtered and the ground spread with salt so it would not be habitable again.

The Colonna Cardinals were later pardoned but Jacopone was sentenced to perpetual imprisonment. Cold, starving, with his legs in chains and deprived of the sacraments, he was lodged in solitary confinement and incommunicado in the bleak dungeon of the city's Castel San Pietro.

In a poem (*Lauda* LV) he describes his cramped and stinking cell, the rats that shared it with him and how little he suffered because he had become so inured to deprivation. Later, he wrote to the Pope accepting his detention as a penance and asking to be allowed the sacraments but simultaneously refusing to accept release on condition that he withdraw his criticism of the Pope.

His petition was rejected and he spent most of his six years incarceration writing some of the one hundred or more poems, some devotional and tender, others sarcastic and scathing, for which he is famous.

Not unnaturally, the sneered-at Pope was infuriated. His antipathy against Jacopone was so strong that the poet was personally excluded from the general amnesty for the Jubilee of 1300, the first such event in Catholic Church history.

Boniface was unmoved by the widespread antipathy towards him. In 1302, he expounded his view of the papacy in the Papal Bull *Unam Sanctam*. In it he declared that it was 'absolutely necessary for salvation that every human creature be subject to the Roman pontiff', the most far-reaching statement of papal supremacy in the Church's history.[2]

The final years of his pontificate were occupied in a feud with King Philip IV (Philip the Fair) of France who had stopped Church funds being sent to Rome. In 1302, as the feud worsened, Philip was excommunicated. He retaliated, in collusion with the Colonna family, by sending an army of two thousand mercenaries to arrest the Pope at his sanctuary in his birthplace in Anagni.

Boniface was beaten up badly and saved only at the last minute from being executed by the Colonna army General. Three days later, he was released when the citizens of Anagni drove the mercenaries out. Humiliated and shocked at this assault on the Vicar of Christ, he died a few weeks later. The rumour was that he had committed suicide from 'gnawing his own arm' or bashing his skull against a wall.

Jacopone was pardoned in 1302 by the next Pope, Benedict XI, who reigned for only nine months. In December the following year he was freed by Benedict's successor, Clement V, a Frenchman and the first of the Popes who quit Rome and were located in Avignon for the next sixty-seven years. Jacopone retired to a Poor Clare convent in the mountain town of Collazone near Todi. To the end he kept up his vigorous advocacy of ascetic poverty and his denunciation of corruption in the Church.

On Christmas Eve, 1306, while he and some of his brethren were in the Poor Clare convent at Collazone, Jacopone knew that his time had come. Like St Francis, he welcomed Sister Death with song: 'I weep because Love is not loved', he said.[3]

For weeks during his final illness, he had rejected all the anxious pleas of his fellow friars to ask for the Last Rites. Just hours before he breathed his last, his closest friend and fellow mystic, Blessed John of La Verna, providentially appeared on the scene and administered the last rites to him. Then Jacopone sang one of his favourite poems 'Jesus, In Thee is all our trust, high hope of every heart.'

When he finished, he closed his eyes and, it was claimed, died from excess of love for the Infant Jesus, just as the priest who was celebrating midnight Mass in the adjoining chapel intoned the *Gloria in Excelsis* ('Glory to God in the highest and on earth peace to men of good will'). He was about seventy-six.

Though he had been ridiculed in his earlier days as a crazed vagrant, by the time of his death Jacopone had become very popular. Among the common people he was customarily called 'Blessed' though he was never officially named as such. He was even highly-regarded by many clerics and especially by the Franciscans who also call him Blessed and have made several unsuccessful attempts to have the Roman Curia accept his cause for canonisation.

In 1433, one hundred and thirty-seven years after his death, Jacopone's remains were removed from the Church of the Poor Clares at Collazone and placed in a magnificent tomb in the Church of San Fortunato at Todi. His Latin inscription translates as:

> The bones of Blessed Jacopone dei Benedetti of Todi, of the Order of Friars Minor, being foolish for Christ, hoodwinked the world with a new skill and stormed heaven. He sleeps in the Lord.[4]

It is a beautiful and apposite epitaph, fully in tune with Jacopone's own opinion of himself as expressed in his poem:[5]

> *Senno me pare e cortesia*
> *Empazir per lo bel Messia.*[6]

Notes

[1]   See T. Oestereich, 'Pope Boniface VIII' in C. G. Herberman, et al., *The Catholic Encyclopaedia* (New York: Robert Appleton Company, 1907), vol. 2, p. 662.

[2]   *Ibid.*, p. 667.

[3]   See Roman Catholic Saints web page: www.roman-catholic-saints.com/blessed-jacopone-of-todi.html.

[4]   Translation mine.

[5]   *Lauda* LXXXIV.

[6]   'Wisdom 'twould seem and courteous behaviour
      To be a fool for the gentle Saviour.' (my translation).

8

THE PROS AND CONS

F ALL THE controversies surrounding the *Stabat Mater*, that of its authorship is the most perplexing. There will continue to be arguments pro and con all contenders though most modern authorities agree that the only two likely candidates are Pope Innocent III and Jacopone da Todi. However, in my estimation, the arguments in favour of the latter are much stronger than those supporting Pope Innocent and I think they justify my conviction that he is the author of the poem. Let me marshal my arguments here.

1. What little is known about the early history of the poem is in favour of Jacopone. First, and most cogent, is the fact that two fourteenth-century manuscripts and a version of the poem published in 1495 name him as the author of the *Stabat Mater*. The latter also lists him as the author of a somewhat similar poem, the *Stabat Mater Speciosa* (of which more later). No similar evidence exists in relation to Pope Innocent III.

2. The *Stabat Mater* was well-known both in and beyond Italy in the final decades of the fourteenth century. The first recorded mention of it was in the Genoese Annals, a sort of diary written by the then Chancellor of Genoa, Georgius Stella, who died in 1420. He mentioned that the *Flagellanti* in his city were singing it in 1388. Other sources spoke of it being in use by the *Albati* and *Bianchi* (White) sodality groups in Provence in 1399.

Innocent III died in 1216, one hundred and seventy two years before the Genoa reference. Even though word of mouth was the customary means of communication at the time, that seems a very long period for a Pope's composition to become recognised.

Jacopone da Todi died in 1306, ninety years after the Pope and just eighty-two years before the 1388 mention. This seems a more reasonable interval for a poem written by him to circulate and it strengthens the argument that he was its author.

3. A poem like the *Stabat Mater,* where the poet demands to share the suffering and degradation of the crucified Christ and his sorrowing mother, is unlikely to be the work of a Pope who is said to have had 'a great and cold intellect' and who claimed precedence over every other ruler in Europe. And, if he had written it, he would certainly have seen that his own poem was promptly made an official part of the liturgy. In fact, it was not inserted into the Roman Missal and Breviary until 1727.

4. One of the most frequently-used arguments against Jacopone's authorship of the poem is that none of the numerous hymns and poems acknowledged to be his are written in Latin. All the rest are written in the craggy Umbrian dialect spoken in a large part of central Italy while the *Stabat Mater* is the only one written in fairly stylish Latin.

Since this argument is regarded by some scholars as conclusive, it is worth examining in some detail. First, the implication that Jacopone was not able to speak educated Latin is totally unconvincing. At the time the poem was written, Latin was—and would still be for four or more centuries—the *lingua franca* of the educated classes throughout most of what is now

Europe. Jacopone was educated in one of the leading law universities in Italy. Earlier in his career, he was an influential lawyer and would certainly have needed to speak and write in Latin.

However, after the death of his wife, he had purposely discarded all that would evoke his previous style of living, especially anything connected with the profession that had profited him in ways he now considered corrupt. Writing in Latin would certainly do that.

5. How, then, did it come about that he is now one of the most likely of those credited with writing the Latin *Stabat Mater* for that honour?

That question has not been answered from the time it was first raised. Judging from the way the answer is becoming more elusive it is not likely to be found soon. That justifies me in putting forward the following conjecture.

After his lengthy period of self-mortification in the Umbrian countryside, Jacopone had been admitted to the Friars Minor, as the Franciscan order was called, some time around 1268.

At the time, the Franciscans were spreading rapidly throughout Europe, their evangelical zeal being far more appealing to ordinary people than the older Benedictine Order's academic approach. As a result, some of the less important Benedictine foundations, including the one at Todi, had fallen into neglect and were taken over by the Franciscans.

As part of their crusading drive, they embarked on a project to promote homage to the Blessed Virgin. For this they needed a propaganda campaign that would be understood in the various countries with different languages in which the Order was established. Latin

was the obvious answer. What better strategy could
there be than to get one of their own to write a Latin
poem that would achieve the desired result?

My theory is that while he was still a relatively new
recruit, Jacopone was summoned by his local superior
and, at his request or, more likely, at his behest, was
invited to write a Latin poem about the Virgin Mary
for the campaign the order was preparing to launch.

Such an approach would have faced Jacopone with
a serious problem. Not only had he turned his back on
Latin while still a layperson but, since being received
into the order, he had rigidly followed the example of
its founder, St Francis.

Francis had died only some forty-two years earlier
at the age of about forty-four. Rejecting his father's life
of luxury, he had devoted himself to the poor. He
expected his followers to live a life of utter poverty,
reclusiveness and humility. He taught that books were
a luxury in a world where the great majority was
illiterate. Latin was the language exclusively of the
upper classes. Only those of his monks who needed it
for studying or writing about theology should use it.

6. Since then, this teaching had divided his later
successors into two camps. The majority of the Todi
friars, mainly the younger members, belonged to the
one that had mitigated the founder's instructions.
Following his death, they had adopted a policy of
active and widespread evangelisation that had proved
more productive than their founder's insistence on a
life of humility, obscurity and poverty. To carry out
their more active leadership role in society they had
found it necessary to acquire property and finances.

Jacopone was one of the minority who disagreed
forcibly with this development. He and others, mainly

older members of the community who felt like him, wanted the strictest adherence to the legacy of the founder. For them, disregard of Latin was part of that.

As time went on, the feud grew more and more bitter, reaching the stage when the earlier members demanded to be allowed to live apart in a different location from the others. Jacopone was to become one of the most forthright advocates of this *Zelanti* (Zealots) wing of the Franciscans and his belligerency in pursuing the cause attracted many and powerful enemies.

However, at the time we are writing about, Jacopone was probably still a relatively new recruit. Though he had refused to be considered for the priesthood, he was now under ecclesiastical jurisdiction. One of the vows a friar took was obedience to a superior.

7. In this scenario, Jacopone was now faced with his prior's suggestion that was effectively an instruction. He might have argued against being asked to write the hymn in Latin. In which case, the prior might remind him that obedience was required of all Friars and that he should be content to use his God-given talent in his Master's cause. If he wished his name to be withheld, that could be arranged.

Because of his vows, no monk would reject such a solution. In Jacopone's position, the anonymity it provided would be doubly welcome. It would diminish the shame he might feel about writing in Latin against his own convictions. It would also shield him against jeers from his Franciscan confrères, both those who supported and those who disagreed with his professed opposition to the use of Latin.

Later chapters will show that he also had supporters and opponents in the Vatican, where he infuriated the Pope to the point that he was excommunicated and imprisoned. If the *Stabat Mater* was written either in his early days in the Order or during the later years, when he had become an extremist mystic, his decision to write the Latin hymn but to accept the concealment of its authorship would be understandable.

To encourage him to comply more willingly with his superior's direction, Jacopone had one more positive enticement. Besides portraying Mary in the sympathetic and sentimental way the Order's campaign would require, he could use it to emphasise humankind's betrayal of its creator and its obligation to atone. Using a more refined Latin version of the language of his earlier poems and more sophisticated rhythm and rhyming arrangements, he could demand punishment for himself and, by analogy, encourage others to adopt a self-punishing regime for themselves. His poem could be an endorsement of and a rallying hymn for the flagellants.

Certainly, while concealing its author's identity, the *Stabat Mater*, with its harsh and highly emotional demands to share in Christ's and Mary's suffering on Calvary, proclaims the same sort of religious extremism Jacopone and his fellow extremists displayed.

It is this combination of conjecture and internal evidence that convinces me that Jacopone was the poem's author. The experts may not accept it as conclusive. But I feel justified in claiming it to be more convincing than any of the claims that have been advanced on behalf of the six saints and Popes that have been mentioned in this context.

8. In my view, however, the two most convincing arguments against the proposition that a Pope or a saint was the author of the poem are based on the text

itself and particularly on the way the poet addresses Mary, the central figure in the poem.

In the first eight of the poem's twenty stanzas, the wording is what might be expected of a distressed but uninvolved spectator on the hill of Calvary two thousand years ago.

In cultured language, he comments on the tragic nature of the event and the apparent ignorance of the onlookers about the appalling nature of the deed they were witnessing. So far that is exactly what a Pope or a saint might be expected to say.

It is in the next nine stanzas that the language changes in a way no Pope or saint would adopt. The literary style of the Latin in these stanzas is much closer to the everyday speech of a brusque small town lawyer than the studied formality to be expected from a Pope or the quiet language of a saint.

Mary is addressed in words that are abrupt and domineering. She is badgered to do this and that as if by a domineering master addressing a servant. Popes and saints are not always known for their finesse and humility but few of them would speak like that.

9. The second, and what I think is the strongest, argument against a Pope or saint being the author of the *Stabat Mater* is a theological one. It applies mainly to Jacopone's closest rival for the honour, Pope Innocent III. It also applies in varying degrees of relevance, to any one of the other two Popes and three saints in the list of possible authors.

The argument is this. Apart from the above contention that no Pope or saint would hector the mother of God in the way the poem does, the poet crosses a doctrinal borderline.

In the nine stanzas in which he directly addresses
her, he brusquely orders her to help him in ways far
beyond the capacity of any mortal. The words he uses
are *Fac* or *Facit* which mean 'Make' or, in this context,
'Make it to happen that… '

She is told to make the poet feel sorrow, make him
to love Christ more, to feel the pain of Calvary, to
divide Christ's suffering with him, to steep him in
Christ's blood.

This tendency to attribute divine powers to Mary has
been popular in the Church down the centuries but has
always been officially rejected. Christian theology does
not regard Mary as divine. However exalted she is as
the Mother of God, she is still a mere mortal.

The Church's teaching is that angels and saints are
worthy of our veneration (*dulia*) and Mary of our
special veneration (*hyperdulia*), but only God is due our
adoration (*latria*). As we pray in the *Gloria* of the Mass:
'For you alone are the Holy One, you alone are the
Lord, you alone are the Most High, Jesus Christ, with
the Holy Spirit, in the glory of God the Father. Amen.'

Mary's role is to act as a mediatrix, an intermediary
or intercessor on our behalf for the graces or miracles we
may desire. And no matter what the crowds at Knock,
Lourdes or Medjugorje may believe, she cannot personally accomplish anything except to ask her Son, as she
did at the wedding feast in Cana, to intervene. It is only
God who can answer such prayers. That is something
every Pope, no matter how much devoted he is to Mary,
as many of them have been, will understand.

10. In my opinion, these are all valid reasons for
maintaining that Jacopone rather than Innocent III or
any of the other clerical contenders should be accepted
as more likely to have been the author of the *Stabat*

Mater. Indeed, I would be tempted to go further and suggest that Jacopone may even have written it specifically for one of the *Flagellanti* groups whose self-punishment practices he seemed to emulate.

Nevertheless, in spite of all those arguments in favour of Jacopone's authorship of the poem, it has to be admitted that in style and content it is very different from the other poems that can be definitively credited to him.

These were known as *Laude* or praise songs and constitute the most interesting part of Jacopone's contribution to the Italian poetry of the final decades of the thirteenth century. More about them in the next chapter.

9

THE PRAISE POEMS

ROM WHAT WE know of Jacopone da Todi, the last thing he would seek was posthumous fame. He had deliberately given up everything he possessed following the tragic death of his wife. The remaining years of his life were spent in uncompromising penance for what he regarded as his sinful past and in promoting the cause of the Franciscan faction that wanted a return to the extreme discipline of the Order's founder.

In one of his later poems (*Lauda* LXXXIV)[1] he said that whoever sought worldly honours was not worthy of the love of the Christ who had died on a cross between two thieves. Shortly before his own death, he refused to recognise the fame he had already acquired, repudiating it as the Devil's temptation.

It was for his copious output of poetry that he became widely known in Franciscan and other clerical circles in the last three decades of the thirteenth century and, in the following centuries, to a wider audience in Europe, particularly when printing became available. More than one hundred poems in the Umbrian dialect have been reliably ascribed to him (though a 1614 edition of his work contains 211 that were all dubiously claimed to be his).

Though many of his poems, particularly the earlier ones, reflect the initial Franciscan emphasis on a life of poverty, simplicity, humility and personal penance, it is a moot point whether it was these ideals or his own

feelings that inspired him more. The fact that most of
the poems attributed to this period are about himself
and his own emotions and reactions suggest that he
and not St Francis of Assisi was his main inspiration.

Nor is it likely that his wife's death was the motivating force for his frequently frenetic outbursts of
emotion. He does mention her obliquely a few times
but his few references to women mainly concern the
danger of their charms as occasions of sin and a
distraction from the ceaseless attention one should be
devoting to God. One of his collected sayings is that
he would just as much notice the face of a beautiful
woman as he would the head of an ass.

The tragedy itself does not feature in his poetry.
Rather it seems to have closed the door on what he
called his earlier 'false life' and allowed him to spend
much of the rest of it in a self-absorbed state that
modern psychotherapists, unfamiliar with thirteenth
century religious mysticism, might diagnose as narcis-
sistic personality disorder.

This harsh speculation is not altogether mine. It
summarises the views of some critics who are more
familiar than I in translating Jacopone's gravelly
Umbrian dialect that admirers of the 'august style' of
the *Stabat Mater's* Latin dismiss as the *volgare*.

There is such a wide variety of themes in his output
and such a variation in his style as he grows older and
his outlook changes that it is impossible to classify him
under any particular label. His literary outpourings—
the only way to describe his voluminous poetry—
range from acerbic and sardonic attacks on people who
annoy or oppose him to the height of mysticism as he
wrestles with his conscience and seeks to unite himself
with Jesus both in his sufferings and in mutual love.

Writers about mysticism divide its development into five stages. The first stage is the awakening, represented in Jacopone's instance by his casting off of his former lifestyle in reaction to the mortification he experienced as a result of his wife's death. The other stages are purgation (of the senses, the will and the spirit); illumination (the beginning of union with God, sometimes accompanied by visions and a feeling of God's presence); the 'Dark Night of the Soul', as St. John of the Cross called it, when God seems to withdraw temporarily; and the final stage of the quest— unity with God.

For Jacopone, each of these stages produces its distinctive poetic mood to match the phase of his religious evolution. The earliest poems are sometimes coarse, vulgar and inelegant. His criticisms are often directed at himself and he confesses his own earlier misdeeds, the worst of which he lists as gambling, usury and cheating the poor. At times, he despairs of being able to lead a good life and even contemplates suicide.

In this first stage of mysticism, Jacopone is preoccupied with sin and death and the thought of an eternity of punishment terrifies him. This fear, fuelled by the lurid polemic of wandering preachers predicting the imminent end of the world, is difficult for present-day Christians to comprehend.

In his biography of Jacopone, *The Fool of God*, the American writer, George T. Peck, singled out three significant movements as the main influences on the poet.

The first of these was the prevalence of self-flagellation, fostered mainly by the religious orders but also by a public outbreak of self-punishment at the time.

In turn, this was the product of a widespread belief that the world was to end in 1260, the probable year of Jacopone's birth. The theory, first advanced by Abbot Joachim of Fiore (1168–1202), was that Adam and Jesus respectively had inaugurated the first and second eras of human existence. The end of the second era was now at hand and the third era of the Holy Spirit taking over and therefore the coming of the Last Judgement was nigh.

Even though the 1260 deadline came and went without the world ending, the apocalyptic terror persisted. As further divisions split the warring Italian city states, an outbreak of penitential marches saw hundreds of thousands of terrified people take to the roads throughout Italy and in countries as far afield as Austria, Germany and France. To encourage and assist the marchers, a spate of marching songs was circulated.

Jacopone's early poems attracted criticism from several quarters, including fellow Franciscans, for his extreme and often offensive views. One poem, addressed to a learned fellow friar who had died, wondered whether his learning had saved him or if he was now 'burning'. But censure did not disturb him. When he was dismissed by some as a madman, he wrote, as mentioned in the previous chapter, that he believed it was right and proper for him to be a fool for Christ's sake.

This may simply be a way of brushing off his detractors or, as Peck concludes, it is the result of Jacopone's 'holy madness', the poet's way of 'stilling the human mind in order to let in the flood of God's love'.

In the second mystical stage of purgation, his poems reflect his efforts to cast off all the associations and attachments of ordinary life. Wealth, esteem and high office are to him worthless. The rich, including some clerics he addresses personally, are corrupt, avaricious and depraved, risking damnation as the poor are left to starve. Scholarship is useless because it favours the elite and distracts one from contact with God who knows our every word and thought. The only way to appease him is through suffering.

One of his poems (*Lauda* XXV) of this period is *Quando t'alegri, omo de altura* (When you rejoice, proud man).[2] This is intended as a warning to a man who, like Jacopone himself had done, is living a life of luxury. The poet takes him to look into the future at his putrefying corpse lying in the ditch. He then conducts a morbid conversation with it, recalling the way the man looked during his life.

Mentioning in turn each part of the body, he describes how beautiful it used to be and asks him how his fine clothes, his neatly combed hair, his eyes and nose and so on, all of which featured in his sinful lifetime, look now. The corpse's revolting descriptions of their present appearance are scarifying, as is obviously the poet's intention.

The poem is too long to quote here in full, but translations, in prose and in poetry, of two linked stanzas may convey an impression of its impact. Peck's prose translation reads:

> Poet: Now, where is your nose that you had to smell with? What hellishness made it fall off? You couldn't help yourself against the worms; your pride is much reduced.

> Corpse: This nose of mine, which I had to smell with, fell off with a great stink. I did not think of this when I was in love with the false world full of vanity.[3]

To illustrate how poetry can enhance the translation, here is my own version of the same two stanzas:

Poet:

Where is the nose that you had for smelling?
The way it fell off you was quite repelling
Worms are now free to make it their dwelling
Your prestige is gone and your vanity

Corpse:

Here is the nose that I had for smelling
The stink it made when it fell was telling
I'd not thought of that when on earth I was dwelling
And living a life of profanity.

This is a modest enough translation but it replicates the metre, the wording and the rhyming arrangement of the original and may give the reader an idea of the impression the poem would have made on its Umbrian hearers seven hundred years ago.

At some time in the final decade of the thirteenth century, a new stage in Jacopone's life began. He was summoned to Rome to become secretary to Cardinal Bentivenga, a native of Todi. Given his convictions about the need for the Franciscans to embrace the Primitive Rule of their founder, it was inevitable that he would become involved in the bitter dispute then being waged between the rival hard line and moderate factions.

By now Jacopone was one of the leaders of the hard-liners. For reasons that had nothing to do with monastic discipline, they were being supported by the Colonna Cardinals and Italian nobility who were trying to force the Pope to resign. It was at this time that Jacopone wrote the poems that made the Pope his enemy for life and resulted in his imprisonment in 1298.

One of these poems (*Lauda* LII)[4] contains a line that needs no translation: *Jesù Christo se lamenta de la Chiesa Romana.* Another (*Lauda* LVIII),[5] addressed personally to Boniface, warns him that he won't die laughing because of his many misdeeds, among which the poet includes greed, theft, pride and even heresy.

It was shortly after it was written that Boniface defeated the Colonna faction that, with Jacopone's support, had challenged the validity of his election and Jacopone was imprisoned. Whether he felt it more diplomatic to do so, or because he became resigned to his incarceration and even to have welcomed it as helping his spiritual growth, Jacopone subsequently toned down his rhetoric. As if acknowledging that he had overstepped the mark, he pleads with the Pope, not for freedom but to annul his excommunication decree and permit him to receive the Sacraments.

In a second direct appeal to Boniface, he repeats his plea and asks the Pope to speak with him and to absolve him even if it meant his having to endure his other punishments for the rest of his life. There is no record of Boniface paying any attention to either appeal.

Though academics argue about precisely when Jacopone wrote a particular poem, it may have been during his six years in prison that he composed what is probably, along with the *Stabat Mater*, his most famous poem, *Donna del Paradiso* (Lady of Paradise)[6] which experts regard as the origin of drama in Italy.

Up to this time, Italian poets had a maximum of two people and the poet himself as *dramatis personae*. In his version of the Calvary story, Jacopone had an extra person, in this instance Mary Magdalene, along with Christ and his mother, a messenger and the crowd in his very moving depiction of the Passion of which a much tamer version is performed in Catholic churches on Good Friday.

In sixty-eight lines, this poem (*Lauda* XCIII)[7] starts with a graphic description of a messenger advising Mary to run quickly because people are scourging her son and acting as if they were going to kill him. Mary cannot understand why they would want to harm someone who was so good. She appeals to Mary Magdalene for help and also to the crowd to spare him.

Each character speaks two or three lines at a time as the tension mounts and Christ is crucified. The poet himself also speaks, telling Mary not to mourn and to help her son's followers. The poem ends with Mary distraught and keening and the messenger saying that what has happened has caused the death of both mother and son.

Peck's English translation of this poem,[8] especially Mary's last lament, conveys how deeply moving the original text must have been to the Umbrian peasant audience. It reads:

> Son, your soul has departed—son of the desolate one
> Son of the beaten one—dead son
> Son, white and rosy—son without compare
> Son, to whom shall I turn—son, now that you have left me?
> Son, white and blond—son with the happy face
> Son, why has the world so disdained you?
> Son, sweet and pleasing—son of the grieving one
> Son, men have treated you badly.

It is the similarity of style and content between this poem and the *Stabat Mater* that strengthens the conviction that Jacopone was the author of both. But the *Stabat Mater*, besides being written in Latin, is not in the same spiritual league as the Umbrian one and, indeed, of most of the other poems in Jacopone's anthology. Though they are frequently autobiographical and, on occasion, tortuously introspective, some of Jacopone's *Laude* poems are intensely devout, reaching heights of mystical expression that the *Stabat Mater* cannot match.

In *Lauda* XC, *Amor de Caritate*,[9] in what can be described only as a torrent of passion, Jacopone cries out the words 'Love, love' seventy times in forty-eight lines. Christ rebukes him for his 'disorder' but he is so outspoken as to retort that Christ himself had submitted to the disorder of being born a human and accepting his crucifixion.

Others of Jacopone's poems believed to have been written in these years explode with such similar intense passion as to provoke doubts in a modern sceptic about his sanity. For example, in *Lauda* LXXXII[10] he accuses Love, meaning Jesus, of besieging him and taking over his five senses of hearing, seeing, tasting, touching and smelling.

In the next poem he goes even further. Addressing 'the love that has killed Love', he prays that it would also kill him and, at the end, he says that anyone drowned in love is mad and does not know where he is or the right path to take. In a perceptive comment about this period in Jacopone's life, Peck writes:

> Dante's voyage (in the *Divine Comedy*) was through an ordered cosmos ruled by human reason and divine love, while Jacopone's was into a chartless infinity entirely beyond human reason. Herein lies the madness of the fool of God.

Nevertheless, the calmer and more moderate style of other poems presumed to be of this period indicates that the sufferings of prison did not thwart his unremitting and seemingly successful efforts to get closer to God and to lose himself in the Divine embrace.

In the next two relatively short periods of his spiritual life, Jacopone experienced the final and, to the ordinary Christian, the most incomprehensible stages of the mystic's development. The first of these is when the God, with whom the mystic has experienced close intimacy, inexplicably and hurtfully seems to withdraw contact. The result is, as mentioned earlier, what St Paul of the Cross (1694–1775) called the 'Dark Night of the Soul', a condition that affected him (Paul) for forty-five years.[11]

Many other mystics, both before and after Jacopone's time, have had the same experience of apparent abandonment by the God who had previously been so close. Among those before him were St Bernard of Clairvaux and St Teresa of Avila. After him were St Thérèse of Lisieux (for eighteen months before her death at twenty-four years of age) and more recently Mother Teresa (on frequent occasions over fifty years, the longest-known such period). From their own testimony it is clear that such dark phases were a bitter blow to the mystics, leaving them feeling forsaken and requiring all their faith and trust to endure and, finally, to overcome.

In the three years between his release from prison in 1303 and his death in 1306, Jacopone reached the pinnacle of his mystical evolution. He now sees that his earlier relentless denunciations of wealth, learning and comfortable living were distractions from what he should have been doing—concentrating on the goodness of God and accepting the status quo as the Divine Will. He realises that the temptation to give up hope can be resolved only by total surrender of his whole being to God and complete absorption in him. He would find peace only by leaving the past to God's mercy and meantime burying himself in God's love.

One of Jacopone's final poems, *Lauda* XCII,[12] *La fede e la speranza*, (Faith and Hope) marks what appears to be the summit of his mystical journey. This is the stage that the late Evelyn Underhill, an English Anglo-Catholic expert on Christian mysticism, calls 'that transcendence to which God invites the Soul'.[13] Jacopone declares that 'the war is over' and that his mind is now so covered by a coat of mail that he cannot be wounded by sin.

He has found the seventh heaven; faith has ceased because he can now see; hope also, because he has found what he desired. Night has been turned into day in perfect love. As Dante was to say in his *Divine Comedy*: *E'n la sua volontade è nostra pace* (And in his will is our peace).[14]

Jacopone's apparent softening of some of his previously-held radical convictions had one unforeseen effect. He was disowned by his former associates in the extremist faction of the Franciscan Spirituals, who condemned him as a traitor and an apostate. However, by the late thirteenth century, they had dwindled in influence and in numbers as papal support had been withdrawn and the great majority of friars had found the conservative approach more effective in their missionary work.

Despite the fact that their emphasis on poverty was closer to their founder's original objectives, the hardline movement eventually collapsed. The effort Jacopone had put into the cause and the ill-treatment he had endured in promoting it had been in vain. Perhaps it needed that acknowledgment to convince him of the truth of the saying that man proposes but God disposes.

Literary critics are still divided in their judgment on the merits of Jacopone's work. Some dismiss it as jargon or argot written by a fool or a madman; others, by far in the majority, rate it as among the greatest of the copious body of Italian poetry, secular and religious, of the Middle Ages.

Probably the fairest thing to say about him is that he should not be judged by the post-Christian incomprehension of the twenty-first century but by the standards of the Italy of the thirteenth and fourteenth centuries, when death and the Last Judgment were looming menaces and the world was expected to end at any moment.

Notes

1   See G. T. Peck, *The Fool of God* (Alabama: The University of Alabama Press, 1980), p. 104.
2   *Ibid.*, pp. 58–59.
3   *Ibid.*, p. 60.
4   *Ibid.*, p. 235 (Index).
5   *Ibid.*, pp. 122, 124.
6   *Ibid.*, p. 132.
7   *Ibid.*, p. 146
8   *Ibid.*, p. 150
9   *Ibid.*, p. 182
10 *Ibid.*, p. 172
11 See p. 55 above.
12 See Peck, *The Fool of God*, p. 183.
13 See E. Underhill, *Jacopone da Todi, Poet and Mystic* (London: J.M.Dent & Sons, 1919), p. 242.
14 See Dante Alighieri, *Paradiso*, Canto III, line 85. Dante began his immortal work only two years after Jacopone's death and thirteen years before his own.

The Middle Ages

HE MIDDLE AGES is the name given to the thousand years between 500 and 1500 AD. This was the period from the collapse of the Roman Empire that had ruled the known world for the previous millennium up to the discovery of the New World and the Protestant Reformation that challenged the Catholic Church's long-standing religious dominance in Europe.

By universal consent, it was one of the most remarkable periods in the world's recorded history. It was an epoch full of wars and famine, scandals and schism, as well as of great achievements in art, literature, sculpture and architecture. During it, Christianity would thrice be torn asunder and modern Europe born.

One man and his poem would seem to be a very insignificant few threads in so varied a tapestry. However, an understanding, however shallow, of this great sweep of time is needed to explain why Jacopone da Todi and the *Stabat Mater* have earned their places in its annals.

The era began in the fifth century as Goths, Vandals, Huns and other pagan tribes from north and west Europe overran the Western Roman Empire, sacking Rome in AD 410 and later setting up their own kingdoms. This early period became known as the Dark Ages. But Roman laws and institutions were extensively retained throughout the continent and Roman

Catholicism remained the only recognised religion for the whole of that one thousand years.

By the mid-point of the millennium in AD 1000, most of Europe's then thirty five million population were living in a comparatively small number of large cities, a larger number of smaller towns, an abundant scattering of rural hamlets of a few hundred families and in solitary homesteads.

Society was said to be divided into clergy who prayed, nobles who fought and peasants who worked. The feudal system, which lasted for most of the millennium, was based on a warrior landholder and the vassals and fiefs who rented their holdings from him, paying with their labour or a share of their crops.

To a degree almost impossible to imagine today, religion permeated all areas of life. The Church enforced laws, imposed taxes, founded hospitals, schools and universities, supported the poor and sheltered pilgrims. To a great extent it was the force that held society together.

The teaching that outside the Church there is no salvation gave it great power over a largely illiterate and superstitious population. As a consequence of generous donations and legacies down the centuries, Church authorities at all levels had acquired large areas of territory all over Europe. The Pope personally owned most of central Italy, an area known as the Papal States.

So the Pope was a powerful temporal ruler as well as the supreme spiritual leader of the continent. Several Popes claimed to have authority over all terrestrial princes, even claiming the right—and sometimes even practising it—to excommunicate Kings and Emperors and release a country's citizens from allegiance to its rulers. This inevitably led to Popes, with their private armies, engaging in wars along with or against the other Italian States and the armies of Spain, France, Germany and even the Holy Roman Empire.

Medieval popes lived shorter lives than most of their modern successors. (In 1978, Pope John Paul I died after only thirty-three days in office.) Jacopone da Todi (1230–1306) lived to see eighteen Popes in his seventy-six-year life span. When he was about eleven, one Pope, Celestine IV, died sixteen days after being elected. At the time, he had not even been ordained a priest though he had earlier been made a Cardinal by his uncle, Innocent IV.

The year 1276, when Jacopone was around forty-six, was known as 'the year of four Popes'. Between 10 January and 8 September of that year, one Pope had died and three new ones had been elected, two of them dying after 153 days and 38 days respectively.

Some of the Church's greatest Popes and some of its worst reigned during these centuries. However, the papacy was such a powerful institution that European kings and noble Italian families continued to bribe or wage war in order to choose a Pope or to have one of their members elected to the office.

Two members of the notorious Borgia family were Popes, three of the Orsinis, four of the dei Santis, four of the Medicis. An indication of the laxity at the highest levels of the Church was the career of Giovanni, the third of the Medici Popes. Born in 1475, he was appointed Cardinal when he was fifteen, elected Pope as Leo X when he was thirty-eight and only afterward was ordained priest and bishop.

During the second half of the millennium, between 1000 and 1520, three schisms split the Church. The first was the East-West schism of 1054, as Pope Leo IX sought to impose Rome's pre-eminence over the Eastern Roman Empire Patriarchates in Constantinople, Antioch, Jerusalem and Alexandria.

When Patriarch Cerularius of Constantinople refused to abandon his right to call himself Ecumenical (or universal) Patriarch, the Pope's legate excommunicated him and was, in turn, excommunicated by the Patriarch. The result was that the Church was divided into the Orthodox and Roman Catholic wings, a split that has lasted to this day.

Three hundred and twenty years later the seeds of another schism were sown. In 1377, Pope Gregory XI, the last of the seven successive French Popes who had moved the papacy to Avignon, returned it to Rome after an absence of sixty-seven years, a period known as the Babylonian Captivity of the papacy. Eight months later, Gregory died and the Roman crowds forced the Cardinals to elect an Italian, Pope Urban VI, to succeed him.

Fearing for their lives, the French Cardinals fled back to Avignon and elected a rival French Pope. This was the beginning of the so-called Western Schism that lasted for thirty-nine years. By that time, there were three competing Popes, each claiming to be the legitimate Pontiff. In 1417, the Council of Constance, which was then in session, ended the dispute by arranging the willing or compulsory resignation of them all and electing Cardinal Oddone Colonna as Pope Martin V.

The ending of the schism did little to purge the papacy and free the Church from its problems. Some of the worst Popes in the history of the Church reigned towards the end of the Middle Ages.

One hundred and fifty years after the Western Schism was brought to an end, the third major rift divided the Western Catholic Church into its present-day configuration of Roman Catholic and Protestant.

With such conflicting interests to serve, the Church at all levels lurched between intervals of extraordinary religious activity and periods of appalling corruption, sometimes both at the same time.

As the millennium came to an end, the Roman Catholic Church, which had presided over Christian Europe for the previous twelve hundred years, stumbled forward, apparently blind to the threatening tragedy ahead.

The Popes at this critical period—Alexander VI, Pius III, Julius II and Leo X—were incapable of meeting the challenge of the times.

Alexander was Spanish, a member of the Borja (Italianised as Borgia) family. He openly kept mistresses and fathered the infamous Lucrezia Borgia.

His successor, Pius III, nephew of Pius II, lasted only twenty-six days in office before dying of a leg ulcer or, possibly, from poisoning.

He was followed by Julius II, who—to illustrate the prevalence of cardinal-nephew nepotism—was the nephew of Sixtus V and uncle of Clement VII. He raised money by granting indulgences to those contributing to the reconstruction of St Peter's, commissioning Michelangelo to paint the Sistine Chapel ceilings.

The last of the four Popes whose reigns spanned the change from the fifteenth century to the sixteenth was Leo X, the second son of Lorenzo ('the Magnificent') Borgia. Living up to the promise he made after his election—'Since God has given us the papacy, let us enjoy it'—he engaged in vast building projects like the great new St Peter's, of which his predecessor, Julius II, had laid the foundation stone seven years earlier.

To raise the money, like many other Popes, he resorted on a grand scale to simony (selling of ecclesiastical appointments) and of permits to run shrines and pilgrimage centres, all of which led the Church into deeper debt.

His main source of finance, however, was the wholesale selling of indulgences that people bought in the belief that they would reduce the time they or their deceased relatives would have to spend in Purgatory. Wealthy donors could get documents signed by the Pope himself in return for their donation.

To increase the proceeds, he put a Dominican friar called Johann Tetzel in charge of selling of indulgences in all of Germany. The friar's promotional slogan is quoted as claiming that 'As soon as a coin in the coffer rings, the soul from purgatory springs.'

At the time, Martin Luther was drafting the ninety-five theses he later sent to the Bishop of Mainz (the story of his nailing them to the door of Wittenberg Cathedral is now discounted). Theses 35 and 36 challenged the way some of the indulgences were being sold with the implied assurance that they would secure pardon for sins not yet confessed and pardoned and even those not yet committed.[1]

Thesis 86 asked this question: 'Why does the pope, whose wealth today is greater than the wealth of the richest Crassus, build the basilica of St Peter with the money of poor believers rather than with his own money?'[2]

Facilitated by the newly-invented printing press, Luther's challenge quickly spread throughout Germany and northern Europe. It was the beginning of the Protestant Reformation that brought about the third schism and the second of the two major divisions in the Church.

By the time Leo X died in December 1521, the Catholic Church in Europe had pretty well split in two. Many unrelated events, such as the Black Death plague, improved education, the invention of the printing press, papal avarice, moral corruption and, finally and most powerfully, the new Western Schism had shattered the Roman Catholic Church and contributed to a ground swell of popular dissatisfaction.

In this fragmentary and superficial account of the Middle Ages, the emphasis has been on the weakness and failings of the Roman Catholic Church and particularly of the papacy. It has not done justice to the way many good Popes tried to clean up the corruption in the Church and especially to stamp out immorality, simony and corruption.

Nor does it detail the origin and expansion, from the sixth century to the eighth, of many monastic foundations, including those established by Irish monks like Columbanus, Gall, Fiachra, Colmcille and many others.

However, it provides a context for the forthcoming chapters that explain the part that, even after his death, Jacopone's poem played in the momentous events that followed.

All in all, the Middle Ages marked some of the highest and lowest points in the Church's chequered history. Of its ten disparate centuries, however, one is regarded as the most newsworthy, though not, perhaps, for the most gratifying of reasons. Welcome to what has been called the Calamitous Century.

Notes

[1]   See http://www.luther.de/en/95thesen.html.
[2]   See *ibid*.

11

THE CALAMITOUS CENTURY

ESPITE MORE THAN half a lifetime of an ascetic existence and six years of incarceration when he was in his late sixties and early seventies, Jacopone da Todi had lived to the age of seventy-six. This was at a time when the worldwide average life expectancy for a male was in the thirties.

As noted earlier, he died on 25 December 1306, at the start of a century that historians agree was the most ruinous of the ten centuries of the Middle Ages. In her book *A Distant Mirror*, the American historian, Barbara Tuchman, fittingly named it the 'Calamitous 14th Century'.[1]

The century's noteworthy events as listed by Tuchman, though not in chronological order, were:

> The Hundred Years' War, the Black Plague, the Papal Schism, pillaging mercenaries, anti–Semitism, popular revolts including the Jacquerie in France, the liberation of Switzerland, the Battle of the Golden Spurs, and peasant uprisings against laws that enforced the use of hops in beer.[2]

Fascinating and instructive as the exercise might be, this is not the place to explore all these historic events. Mention has already been made of the Papal or Western Schism but of the other historic occurrences that Tuchman lists only two—the Black Plague and anti-Semitism—are directly relevant to the *Stabat Mater* story. The next two chapters are devoted to them.

For Europe, the century's problems began in 1315 when the whole northeast of the continent was stricken by a plague that killed one tenth of the population. Three years of torrential rain were followed by a long period of bad weather and poor crops. This marked the beginning of what history knows as the Little Ice Age that saw Europe's temperature drop by an average two degrees for five centuries.

This early plague was called the Great Famine. In reality, it was only a very mild foretaste of the horrendous pandemic that struck some thirty years later. Over the following four centuries it would afflict almost every part of the European continent. It came to be known as the Black Death.

There are two theories, one grimmer than the other, about how it reached Europe. The conventional belief is that it came with a camel caravan bringing goods from China down the Silk Road to the Crimean port of Caffa, now Feodosiya. Here, Genoese merchants, who had trading rights in the city, loaded the goods on to twelve galleys for transport to ports in Sicily, Italy and France.

The second theory is that when the camel caravan arrived in the Crimea, Caffa had been enduring a prolonged siege by a Mongol army that was already infected with the plague. To get rid of their own dead and in order to infect the defenders in the city, the Mongols were said to have catapulted thousands of putrefying corpses over the walls. The Genoese galleys put out to sea as soon as possible but not before their own crewmen had been contaminated.

Whatever the immediate cause, the fact was that the ships' black rats had been colonised by a hitherto unknown strain of the camel train's Oriental fleas that were carrying the deadly disease. The first of the Genoese ships discharged at Constantinople, where soon five thousand deaths a day were counted, eventually resulting in the loss of forty per cent of the citizens. The next unloaded at Sicily and the whole island was soon affected.

The other galleys soon put into the Italian ports of Naples, Genoa, Venice and Pisa, landing their deadly cargoes. The last of them arrived in Marseille, France's second largest city, where fifteen thousand of its twenty-five thousand population were to die.

At first, the connection was not made between the ships' flea-ridden rats and the deaths. But soon, some coastal cities banned ships from docking and it was reported that if an oarsman coughed he was immediately thrown overboard to prevent the disease spreading. Other reports told of galleys arriving in port with dead and dying men at the oars. One ship, with every one of the crew dead, drifted off the Norwegian coast until it beached in Bergen.

The disease spread with alarming speed. By the middle of 1348, it had covered the southern half of France and spread into Spain, Portugal and England. Then it turned north, reaching as far as Greenland and east through Germany and Poland as far as Russia and North Africa.

Some parts of Europe were hit worse than others. In southern France, Spain and Italy, as many as fifty to eighty per cent of the population is believed to have died. In Avignon in southern France, where the papacy was then installed, officials calculated that three-quarters of the total population died in the first eight months. The death toll was sixty-two thousand citizens, including nine Cardinals.

Germany fared far better than most other European countries, though death tolls in Hamburg and Bremen were sixty to seventy per cent of their inhabitants. However, just 1,244,413 deaths, or twenty per cent of the total, were listed among all of Germany's dead.

Ireland, too, escaped the worst of the plague though the east and south coast ports and the main towns in the Pale were affected. Most of the deaths were of Norman and English colonists and were so severe that special provisions had to be made in the 1366 Statute of Kilkenny to make sure former Irish owners did not get a chance to repossess their lands.

A Brother John Clyn was the only person left alive in Kilkenny's Franciscan monastery. Before he too died he wrote: 'I leave parchment to continue this work, if perchance any man survive and any of the race of Adam escape this pestilence and carry on the work which I have begun.'[3]

England was particularly badly hit. The first appearance of the plague was in London in the autumn of 1348 and by the following summer the whole country was affected. By 1400, England's estimated pre-plague population of seven million had been reduced to two million, a fall of seventy per cent. When the plague broke out again in London in 1563, Queen Elizabeth I moved her court to Windsor Castle where she erected gallows and ordered that anyone coming from London was to be hanged.

Scotland was unlucky. Because of its relative remoteness it might have escaped the plague altogether. But it chose the wrong time, when England's armies were fighting in France in the Hundred Years War, to send a twelve thousand-strong force into England to fight for Scottish independence. Not only were the Scots beaten in battle by a force England had secretly kept at home for just such a possibility but many of those who survived brought the infection home with them.

The symptoms of the disease were both alarming and disgusting. The fleas punctured the victim's skin and, engorged with blood, lodged in the victim's lymph nodes. These swelled into large, painful blisters or buboes (hence bubonic) usually in the legs, groin, armpits or neck. These grew to be the size of an egg or an apple and oozed blood and pus.

Other symptoms were intestinal bleeding, fever and lethargy. Gangrene showed as dead black blood on and under the skin and the nails. The fevered victims suffered severe pain and died quickly between two and four days after infection.

As the disease spread, it got worse and new symptoms developed. Lungs were affected and the feverish victims coughed continuously and bled repeatedly before dying in one to three days. Instances were cited of people going to bed well and dying in their sleep and of doctors being contaminated by the patient and dying on the spot.

Inevitably, it was in the congested cities with their overcrowded tenements and fetid sewers that the death toll was greatest. Hindsight suggests that the plague would have been considerably less destructive if the peasants, who formed the majority of the population of Europe in the fourteenth century, had remained where they were and kept away from one another as much as possible.

Instead they abandoned their small villages, the safest places to be, and packed into the towns and the cities where the initial risk of infection was highest and the crowded conditions made things even worse.

Those who stayed at home made the same understandable mistake of seeking companionship, either for assistance or as refuge from the terror. Even their animals were affected by the disease and hundreds of thousands of pigs, sheep, cows and chickens died, adding to the terrible consequences of the pandemic.

One of the main problems was that ignorance of the cause of the disease meant that no remedies for it were available. In England, specially recruited though unqualified doctors, wrapped head to toe in full-length robes and hoods and wearing leather gloves and boots, had nothing stronger than herbs such as rose, lavender, sage and bay. Stomach pains were treated with wormwood, mint, and balm and lung problems with liquorice.

Another problem was disposal of the thousands of corpses of the victims. When graveyards filled up, bodies were dumped into twenty feet deep plague pits that were enlarged as required. Horrifying stories were told of parts of bodies surfacing or being dug out and eaten by starving dogs. Often bodies were simply thrown into the rivers. Parents abandoned their dying children and children their parents. Householders were told to put their dead outside the house for collection each morning.

The plague was at its worst between 1348 and 1351. Over the next four centuries it returned several times for shorter periods, breaking out in one European city or another—Paris (on many occasions), Amsterdam, Venice, Vienna, Naples, Seville, London (several times), Helsinki, Stockholm, Marseilles, Moscow— each attack persisting for two to three years at a time before moving on somewhere else. One of its final eruptions was the Great Plague of London (1665–1666) in which one hundred thousand people are believed to have died.

The Black Death was one of the greatest catastrophes in recorded history and its final death toll is still disputed. A minimum number of deaths is twenty million, though the latest estimates put the European total at fifty to seventy million, some one-third of the population. Millions more died in the subsequent recurrences of the plague until it died down in the nineteenth century. In all, the world death toll has been estimated at one hundred and fifty five to two hundred and twenty million out of an estimated overall total population of five hundred million. It took Europe one hundred and fifty years to recover from the economic and societal havoc the plague caused.

It was not until 1895, almost five hundred and fifty years later, that the organism that caused the plague was identified by the French bacteriologist, Alexandre Yersin. Hence its technical name Yersinia pestis or simply Y. pestis. More recently, it has been suggested that it may have been a plague of viral haemorrhagic fever, similar to Ebola, carried by humans.

The pandemic itself died out in the late fifteenth century though sporadic outbreaks, causing further deaths, broke out here and there for another four hundred years until it left Europe in the nineteenth century.

Readers may wonder what Jacopone da Todi and the *Stabat Mater* had to do with a disease that did not appear in Europe until forty years after the poet's death. That is the theme of the next chapter in this account of the calamitous fourteenth Century.

Notes

1   See B. Tuchman, *A Distant Mirror: The Calamitous 14th Century* (New York: Alfred A. Knopf, 1978), Title Page.
2   Tuchman, *A Distant Mirror*.
3   See F. White, 'The Plague, or Black Death, in Ireland' in Times Past column in *The Nationalist*, Carlow (19 November 2014).

12

THE POGROMS

HE BLACK DEATH had struck Christian Europe at a time when the Roman Catholic Church was particularly vulnerable to censure. The papacy was in the middle of the so-called Babylonian Captivity that lasted from 1309 to 1377. For those sixty-seven years, seven consecutive French Popes, under pressure from their country's rulers, deserted Rome and had transferred the papacy to Avignon in southern France.

In January 1348, the plague reached Avignon. The reigning Pope for the previous six years was Clement VI, a Benedictine. When he consulted his astronomers on what had caused the disease, they told him it was the result of a rare conjunction of the planets Jupiter, Saturn and Mars several years previously. For his own safety, he was advised to remain in his chambers with a fire and torches burning night and day to keep the plague away.

His medical advisers blamed the plague on a miasma that had poisoned the air. His theological experts were certain it was God's punishment for the way so many people were disobeying the Church and its earthly leader.

If anyone should have been blamed for inviting divine anger it was the Pope himself. On being elected, he had promised to have a good time, saying; 'My predecessors did not know how to be Pope'. He and

the nineteen Cardinals in his court lived lives of luxury
and decadence.

The plague put an end to the high life. It shocked
the Pope deeply and he devoted himself to organising
care for the living and burials for the dead. He ordered
burial pits to be dug all over the city and when no more
land was available he consecrated the Rhone and
ordered bodies to be thrown into it.

And when he was told that victims were dying in
terror or cursing the Church because there were not
sufficient priests left alive or willing to risk adminis-
tering the last rites, he gave laymen—'and even
women if necessary'–permission to officiate at funerals
and even to absolve penitents. Finally, he granted a
plenary indulgence to all who confessed their sins.

As the plague spread further throughout Europe,
ordinary people, terrified by what they saw all about
them, reacted in contrasting ways. Many of them,
fearing that God had deserted his people and was
exacting retribution for their sins, turned despairingly
to extremes of religion. Commonsense was abandoned. Many of them resorted to physical self-punishment and religious fanaticism took control.

Others reacted in the opposite way. Having lost
faith in a God that would visit such horrors on his
people or would not act to protect them, they jettisoned
all hopes of salvation. Terror-stricken, they abandoned
themselves to a lurid bout of frenzied promiscuity and
depravity of all kinds.

Whatever their behaviour, both groups agreed on
one thing and their instinctive reaction was almost
unanimous. It was to wreak vengeance on whomso-
ever or whatsoever had been the cause of their misery.
They looked for scapegoats and, as is usually the case,

they soon found them—beggars, gypsies, lepers and, particularly, Jews.

Throughout their long history, Jews have observed strict rules about hygiene, especially the washing of hands. Seeing how the Jews, fearing contamination, avoided the wells, the unlettered and crazed peasants were encouraged to believe the Jews had poisoned them. Within a few months a Europe-wide pogrom was launched against them.

The first massacre directly related to the plague was in Toulon, France. In April 1348, an angry crowd ransacked the Jewish quarter, killing some forty Jews in their homes.

Five months later, the Jews in Chillon, near Montreux on Lake Geneva, were burned to death en masse. They were said to have confessed under torture that they had poisoned the wells to wipe out the Christians.

Like the plague itself, the pogrom soon spread west to Spain and east to Germany, Austria and Italy with appalling results. Some horrific reports were circulated about hundreds of Jews being burned to death in specially constructed wooden enclosures, while their infants were pulled from the flames and baptised as Christians.

The Jewish History website, with what in the circumstances is remarkable impartiality, lists the main events like this:

> In January 1349, the entire Jewish community in the city of Basel was burned at the stake. The Jewish communities of Freiburg, Augsburg, Nürnberg, Munich, Königsberg, Regensburg and other centres, were either all exiled or burned. In Worms, in March 1349, the entire Jewish community committed suicide. In Cologne, the Jews were forced to flee.

In Mainz, which had the largest Jewish community in Europe, the Jews defended themselves
against the mob and killed over 200 Christians.
Then the Christians came to take revenge. On
one day alone, on August 24, 1349, they killed
6,000 Jews in Mainz.

Of the 3,000 Jews in Erfurt, none survived the
attack of the Christian mobs. By 1350, those
Jews that survived the Black Death itself were
destroyed by the ravages of the mobs. The
Jewish communities in Antwerp and Brussels
were entirely exterminated in 1350. There were
almost no Jews left in Germany or the Low
Countries by 1351.[1]

From the beginning, Pope Clement VI condemned the
pogrom in the strongest terms. Two months after the first
massacre in 1348, he issued the first of two Papal Bulls
(6 July and 26 September) denouncing the killings.[2] He
declared that Christians themselves had been 'seduced
by the liar, the devil' to blame the Jews who also had
died from the plague.

He ordered the clergy and laity to stop the barbarity
and to protect the Jews. His words and similar rulings
by three other Popes after him were ignored and it was
reported that in some cities where the atrocities had
taken place bishops were among the leading agitators.

It was around this time that the flagellant self-
punishment movement, dormant for many years, came
spontaneously back into action.

Despite periodic Vatican condemnation and sup-
pression, the movement had remained intermittently
active throughout the eleventh, twelfth and thirteenth
centuries. Smaller famines, plagues and crop failures
had taken place during those centuries, stirring up
occasional outbursts. Even Pope Alexander IV's rigor-

ous ban on the movement in 1261 failed to suppress it. But it was in the fourteenth century, after the onset of the Black Death, that it reached its peak, especially between 1349 and 1399.

For the best part of a century, starting in northern Italy, groups of men, and sometimes women, wandered the countryside dressed in white robes or (the men) bare-backed. These bands had names like *Flaggelanti, Battenti, Bianchi,* (Scourgers, Beaters, Whites) and other such titles describing how they acted or were dressed.

Headed by bearers carrying crosses, torches and large banners identifying their group, they took to the roads. Disregarding all extremes of weather, bands of up to ten thousand marched through the countryside singing. One faction, called the Brotherhood of the Flagellants, claimed a membership of eight hundred thousand.

In their hands the most fanatical of them carried chains or ropes with pieces of broken glass or sharp metal attached to whip their backs until they were covered in blood. In this way they believed their self-inflicted punishment would atone for their sins and the sins of the world that merited the anger of a God who was punishing them by ruined crops, wars and diseases.

The marchers' leaders—each group had its own domineering Master—maintained that they were no longer subject to ecclesiastical jurisdiction. They claimed that they had no need for priests to administer the sacraments as they themselves had the power to consecrate the bread and wine, to forgive sin and even to work miracles. They declared that their movement would last for thirty-three and a half years as Jesus' life had.

At first, the Church tolerated the movement and towns and cities on the route welcomed the marchers and provided them with food. But they soon began to be blamed for bringing the plague with them. Eventually they were avoided or driven away when, in their excess of emotion, they murdered priests, monks and ordinary Catholics, claiming they were not sufficiently penitent or were in league with the devil.

Despite official opposition from Rome, the movement spread spasmodically over large parts of Central and Northern Europe, though it never came as far as Britain or Ireland. In some parts of Germany, their fanaticism got so far out of control that they drove out or killed all the Jews in the area, executing Catholics whom they regarded as insufficiently penitent.

One group of German flagellants predicted the end of the world in 1369 but its leader, Konrad Schmidt, was burnt at the stake by the Inquisition. Still his followers persisted and, in 1414 and 1416, two German groups of two hundred and three hundred members respectively were condemned and burned to death. Other trials where the accused were condemned as flagellants were recorded as late as the 1480s.

Some of the songs or hymns the flagellants used as they trudged along the roads of Europe have survived. Not surprisingly, the *Stabat Mater*, which had been written at least fifty years before the pogrom commenced, was among them. Its vivid portrayal of Christ's suffering and his mother's anguish would be sufficient in itself to inflame the marchers. Their fury would be aggravated by their conviction that the same 'perfidious Jews' who, according to the Church's traditional teaching, had caused the Crucifixion were also the cause of the plague and its terrible consequences.

As the plague came around again and again and the flagellants continued to defy Rome, the Church faced them head on. Accusing them of heresy and thus subjecting them to the jurisdiction of the Inquisition, Gregory XI again condemned them in 1372 and instructed the secular authorities to suppress them.

Finally, in the fifteenth century the Inquisition moved to eliminate them altogether. Faced with a crusade against it, the leaders of the movement accepted Church discipline.

Vestiges of the flagellants' penitential practices still survive in Europe and in Central and South America and the Philippines. Some modern members of monastic orders and of Opus Dei also practise a mild form of self-flagellation. This usually involves scourging themselves with a whip of knotted cords called a 'discipline' or wearing a goat-hair or sharp metal band called a 'cilice' under their clothes as a protection against impurity.

The history of the Black Death and the pogrom that it provoked helps to explain why the *Stabat Mater* became so popular and spread so quickly through the Europe of the late Middle Ages.

It also confirmed my original convictions about the poet's reasons for creating it in the first place, what effect he wanted it to have and how he intended to achieve that result. At least I was now satisfied that his first aim was to use it as a means of expressing his own extremist views on self-punishment and his need to atone for what he considered his own failings.

Secondly, I was certain that his main objective was to make his audience feel so guilt-ridden on hearing the poem as to want to inflict punishment on themselves. This suggests that he himself was a flagellant at heart if not an active self-punisher.

Thirdly, I believed the poet chose a particular metre, an abundance of rhyme and a passionate choice of words as his method of achieving that aim. He himself did not live long enough to realise that his work might come to be associated with a dreadful pogrom that would sully the name of Christianity.

The great irony in the whole fourteenth century history of poem, plague and pogrom was that, had Christians learned from Jews the importance of hygiene, the disastrous consequences of the Black Death would possibly have been averted. Hundreds of thousands of lives, both Christian and Jewish, could have been saved and the Calamitous Century spared some of the opprobrium it has rightly earned.

Notes

[1]   See website www.jewishhistory.org/the-black-death.
[2]   See J. J. Norwich, *The Popes* (London: Vintage Books, 2012), p. 208.

13

THE TRANSLATOR'S IDEAL

 HEN COMMENCING MY own English translation of the *Stabat Mater*, I was reassured by the experts' calculation that up to sixty per cent of English words derive from Latin. The obvious corollary would seem to be that translation from Latin into English would be comparatively straightforward.

Even before I started the actual translation, however, I came across three websites that should have made me think twice. One quoted Dr Philip Schaff, a nineteenth century Protestant theologian. His conclusion was: 'The secret of the power of the *Mater Dolorosa* (his title for the *Stabat Mater*) 'lies in the intensity of feeling with which the poet identifies himself with his theme, *and in the soft, plaintive melody of its Latin rhythm and rhyme, which cannot be transferred to any other language.*'[1]

American translator Lawrence Venuti, in his book *Translation changes everything*, states his 'skepticism as to whether cross-cultural understanding is possible in literary translation, particularly when the source text is produced in a remote historical period. 'Archaic poetic forms,' he added, 'cannot be easily imitated in English.'[2]

Another Internet site was more succinct and even more explicit. It quoted the comment of a Russian-born linguist who firmly declared that 'poetry by definition [is] untranslatable.'[3]

Nevertheless I ploughed on. The terms of reference for the self-imposed challenge facing me were now clear. Expressed as a Civil Service draftsman might, they were these:

> Produce for a twenty-first century English speaking readership a translation of a poem written in Latin in an unusual metre and with a complicated rhyming scheme by a thirteenth century extremist Franciscan friar and later used by marching bands of self-flagellating peasants engaged in a pogrom against people they considered to be the cause of one of the worst plagues the world has ever known.

Put like that, the enterprise sounded rather daunting.

The Oxford Companion to the English Language explains translation as 'the communication of the meaning of a source-language text by means of an equivalent target-language text.'[4]

In simpler terms, the translator's function is to provide an interpretation that conveys to new recipients the same meaning and feelings as it had to the original ones.

A successful translator will meet three minimal requirements. The first is a good knowledge of the source language, which in this case is Latin. Second is a very good knowledge of the receiving or target language, as it is called. The third requirement for a translator is a sound understanding of the subject matter of the original text. I convinced myself that I scraped through on all three counts and proceeded with my self-appointed task.

Translators have two main choices as to how they approach their work. One is to translate the text literally from the original or source language into the corresponding words in the second or target language.

The conventional way favoured by most translators is a paraphrase or sense-for-sense translation. This is where the translator seeks to convey the meaning and mood of the original text, rather than just a literal translation of the words.

However, I had chosen the less conventional method in the belief that the more faithfully I reproduced the poet's original text, metre and rhyming scheme, the more accurately I would capture the power and appeal of his poem and communicate the message he wanted to convey.

Perhaps if I had heeded the wisdom of the Russian poet, Yevgeny Yevtushenko, I would have had second thoughts. His view was that 'Translation is like a woman. If it is beautiful, it is not faithful. If it is faithful, it is most certainly not beautiful.'[5]

Looking back, I now realise that though I had anticipated some difficulties I had underestimated them. The first was the discovery that translation from any one language to another is difficult and particularly from Latin, or the Romance languages that developed from it, to English.

Second, translating poetry from one language into poetry in any other language is much harder than translating prose.

And, finally, translating Latin verse into English verse while retaining the meaning, the metre and the rhyming system is the most difficult exercise of all, especially if both metre and rhyming systems are so unfamiliar as those of the *Stabat Mater* are.

Despite the linguistic similarities between the two languages, the structural differences between Latin and English are substantial. Latin is a highly inflected language so that words in a sentence alter frequently and markedly to indicate a grammatical change, such as the gender, case or tense.

Such latitude gives Latin speakers great scope for variety, especially since, as grammarians inform us, Latin has three distinct genders, seven noun cases, four verb conjugations, six tenses, three persons, three moods, two voices, two aspects and two numbers.

One noun might have as many as seven different endings depending on its function in the sentence. The root word remains but its function is demonstrated by a suffix that rhymes with the suffixes of other nouns that have a similar function. The result is that Latin has a lot of rhyming word endings, making it a more difficult language for a beginner to learn but a boon for a vernacular poet looking for rhymes.

English is not heavily inflected. It avoids the need for changes in the root word by using the definite (the) and indefinite (a, an) articles, pronouns like I, you, he, she, and prepositions (of, by, to, etc.) to express different functions. That makes the language easier to learn but much poorer in rhymes, a big disadvantage for the translator.

There is another important difference between the two languages that has a major effect on the translation of poetry. Every syllable in a Latin word is pronounced equally strongly while in English unstressed words like the definite and indefinite articles, propositions and even syllables in words like choc'late and cam'ra are swallowed up or, to use technical language, suffer 'vowel reduction'. The result of this is that more syllables can be fitted into the line while maintaining the metre.

A third difference between Latin and English is the order of words in a sentence. Latin is what is called a free-word-order language, meaning that the words of a sentence can be arranged in almost any order and the meaning will still be clear. This makes it much easier for a Latin poet to construct lines or phrases in such a sequence that they end with words that rhyme.

English is a fixed-word-order language, meaning there is normally only one way of writing or saying a sentence. Obviously this limits greatly the translator's latitude to adopt the style, the metre and, especially, the rhyming scheme of the original.

Still another factor in translating Latin to English is that the only vowel sounds in Latin are A, E, I, O and U, in both long and short forms, so rhyming words are consequently more frequent in that language. An English translator, while he has a bigger variety of vowel sounds (at least twenty) at his disposal, is at a disadvantage.

This may seem to be contradictory. The explanation is that the more numerous the number of vowel sounds that words can end in, the fewer are those that rhyme. English, with its many vowel sounds and very limited number of inflections, is particularly lacking in this regard, while Latin and the Romance languages, with their abundant inflections and fewer vowel sounds, abound in them.

In the case of the *Stabat Mater* this means that the English translator will find it almost impossible to replicate the repetitive rhyming that is one of the most striking features of the Latin poem.

The combination of the wording, the rhythm and the rhyme, sheathed in sonorous polysyllabic Latin words, give the *Stabat Mater* the mesmeric effect on the listener that is a major part of what entitles it to the acclaim it has enjoyed over the centuries.

Notes

1   Italics mine. See H. Henry, 'Stabat Mater' in *The Catholic Encyclopedia* (New York: Robert Appleton Company, 1912), vol. 14, as found on http://www.newadvent.org/cathen/14239b.htm.
2   See L. Venuti, *Translation changes everything* (Abingdon: Routledge, 2012), Chapter 4: Translating Jacopone da Todi, pp. 80–81.
3   R. Jakobson, 'On Linguistic Aspects of Translation' at www.translationdirectory.com/articles/article1667.php.
4   See T. McArthur, ed., *The Oxford Companion to the English Language* (Oxford: Oxford University Press, 1992 edition), p. 1051.
5   See the website www.brainyquote.com/quotes/authors/y/yevgeny_yevtushenko.html.

14

THE CHALLENGE AHEAD

S IT IS for any composer, the first task for the poet of the *Stabat Mater* would have been to decide which of the poetic techniques he would employ in writing his poem. His choice would depend on what he wanted the poem to achieve.

One object was self-evident. It was to express his own emotional feelings about the Crucifixion and the effect the sufferings of Christ and his mother had on him as well as his burning desire to share in them himself.

His second reason, if my interpretation of his motivation is correct, was to excite the same sort of emotions in his listeners and readers so that they too would feel compelled to engage in self-punishment.

The main elements he uses are the metre, the rhyming scheme and the choice of words. The way these are interwoven from the very first stanza throughout the whole poem is masterly and is what gives the *Stabat Mater* its powerful impact on the reader or listener. This is the clearly the intention of the poet.

The insistent metre and the smooth flow of mellifluous rhyming words contribute a great deal to the impression the poem makes on the average reader. The impact is even more compelling on people reciting or singing it. The thumping rhythms seem to mesmerise them and the luscious Latin rhyming words remain lodged in their memories—features that support my theory that the poem was written specifically for a band of marching singers before printing was invented.

How the poet used his command of metre, rhyme and text to create these effects is worth exploring more closely.

1. *The Metre*

The *Stabat Mater* is a poem of 20 three-line stanzas written in trochaic tetrameter. A tetrameter is a line of four feet. Trochaic means that each foot is a trochee — that is a long or stressed syllable followed by a short or unstressed one, e.g. FATH-er.

Trochaic metre is eminently suited to the Latin language where the stress is usually on the first syllable of a two-syllable word and on the strongest syllable in longer words. Because of its structure, English is much more comfortable with a metre where the iamb — a short or unstressed syllable followed by a long or stressed one, e.g. de-CIDE — is predominant. Its use results in a slower pace, perhaps more in keeping with the English temperament.

It was no surprise, therefore, to find that among the 648 poems in my 2002 edition of Palgrave's *Golden Treasury*[1] and the 822 in the 1999 edition of *The Oxford Book of English Verse*[2], or even as far back as the schoolbook 1935 edition of Methuen's *An Anthology of Modern Verse*[3] with some two hundred and fifty entries, I could locate not one poem in which a trochaic metre was used throughout and very few where it was used in even a single line.

How much the choice of metre can determine the atmosphere or mood of a poem may be illustrated by the following comparison. Take for instance these lines in Felicia Hemans' poem *Casabianca*:[4]

The boy stood on the burning deck
Whence all but he had fled;
The flame that lit the battle's wreck
Shone round him o'er the dead.

Written in iambic metre, these lines create a message that seems somewhat offhand and lacking the sense of urgency the story would seem to demand. In trochaic metre, it would sound more high-priority as:

Stood the boy on deck aburning
While the craven crew were turning
Tail as fast as they could go

The calming effect of the iambic metre is more suitable for tranquil verse like Wordsworth's *I wandered lonely as a cloud*[5] or Milton's meditative *When I consider how my life is spent.*[6]

The only comparatively well-known English language poems in trochaic metre are the work of two American poets. One is Edgar Alan Poe's extraordinary *The Raven;*[7] the other is Longfellow's *The Song of Hiawatha*[8] published in 1855. So unaccustomed were Americans to this unusual metre that both these poems, which are now regarded as classics, were at first ridiculed by the critics and parodied by other poets.

The opening lines of the shorter version of the latter poem give an idea of the effect of the unfamiliar trochaic metre:

By the shores of Gitche Gumee
By the shining Big-Sea-Water
Stood the wigwam of Nokomis
Daughter of the Moon, Nokomis
Dark behind it rose the forest
Rose the black and gloomy pine-trees
Rose the firs with cones upon them
Bright before it beat the water
Beat the clear and sunny water
Beat the shining Big-Sea-Water

In English this comes across as somewhat artificial whereas, if translated into Latin, the rhythm would be natural, whatever about the meaning. Older Catholics will be familiar with this trochaic metre in the *Pange Lingua / Tantum Ergo* hymn. Even older Catholics may remember it from the *Dies Irae* which was dropped from the funeral liturgy after Vatican II bishops found it too negative. Children know it in rhymes like *Twinkle, Twinkle Little Star*,[9] where the metre seems to liven the verse up and make the words easier to remember.

Among the handful of other places where I came across versions of it were in Thomas Moore's *Hark! The Vesper Bell is Stealing*[10] and two popular songs, *Lili Marlene*[11] and *Won't you Buy my Pretty Flowers?*[12]

2. The Rhyme

For the poet writing in Latin, bent on composing a hymn for an illiterate peasant audience, rhyme was an important poetic tool. The poet of the *Stabat Mater* uses it primarily to create a mood of poignancy, of horror and distress and of strong determination to suffer alongside Christ and Mary. Where the poet addresses Mary directly, it imparts an atmosphere of impatient demand that is surprising in the circumstances.

Rhyme also acts as a tool to help drive the poem's message home by the choice of words that resonate in a way that makes the lyric itself memorable. The poet uses it liberally, making full use of the inflections in the Latin language that result in many words ending in the same rhyming syllable.

It is also his tool for both inflaming and comforting those speaking or listening to the words and to attract their empathy. And in a time when there were no hymn-sheets, it served as a very useful mnemonic, helping them to remember where they were in the poem and to recall the words.

For both the original poet and the English translator, the wording of the poem is the most amenable of its three main poetic elements. While both metre and rhyming scheme are inflexible, the wording has the important advantage of being variable. This gives poet and translator more freedom of choice in selecting the words they want and in how they are used whereas they have none if they adhere to the rhythm and rhyming systems.

The system of rhyming the Latin poet uses is somewhat exceptional but not unique. What it requires is that the last word in each of the first two lines in each stanza should rhyme. Not just that but also that the last syllable of these two words has to be soft (i.e. unstressed). In addition, the last word of the third line in each pair of stanzas has to rhyme as well as to end in a hard (stressed) syllable. The technical description of this arrangement is AAB CCB.

It may seem very complicated. What it means is that the result will be something like this:

> As you read this explanation
> You will find elucidation
> Of the Stabat Mater hymn
> Rhyme and rhythm, words and metre
> All unite to sound much sweeter
> Cherubim and Seraphim

The attentive reader will have noticed an anomaly in the last line of each stanza. The two other lines are of four trochaic feet, amounting to eight syllables while the final line drops the last light or short syllable. The technical notation for this is 8.8.7. The effect is to end each stanza with a strong emphasis, making the line easier to remember, a boon to people in a pre-Gutenberg age.

It is also helpful for the English language translator who is already in difficulty in keeping to the unaccustomed metre, missing the abundance of rhymes that Latin's generous inflection system provides and lacking the older language's ability to change the order of a sentence without confusing the reader. Ending the stanza with a stressed syllable makes things easier in English with its preference for the iamb over the trochee.

My study of the *Stabat Mater* had convinced me that the poet had a calculated reason for his lavish use of the polysyllable rhyming words throughout his poem. So, as soon as I had finished the final draft of my own translation, I looked for the key to discovering his technique. I found it by comparing the number of multi-syllable words in the Latin poem against the numbers in my own version and those of the four most important existing English translations.

The first result gave me the number of times he included an extra two rhyming words in a stanza in addition to those already demanded by the poem's rhyming scheme. The total was just four. My own score was nil and the scores of the other four English language translators I compare with my own were 0, 6, 4 and 1 respectively. Nothing startling in that.

The next step was to count the number of poly-syllable words in the Latin text even if they did not rhyme with one another in the same stanza. The results were now much more enlightening.

In the best-known English translation (Caswall) there are 7 three-syllable words and only 1 four-syllable word in a total of 316 words.

In the three other familiar English translations the scores were: Bulman twenty words of 3 syllables and eight of 4 syllables in a total of 345 words;[13] MacCarthy seven of 3 syllables and six of 4 syllables in a total of 363 words;[14] and Collegeville seven of 3 syllables and nine of 4 in a total of 351 words.[15] My own score was thirteen 3 syllable words and seven of 4 syllables in a total of 364 words.

By comparison, the Latin text has a total of only 217 words. Into it the poet has crowded forty-one words of 3 syllables, nineteen of 4 syllables and even two words of 5 syllables. This preference—an English translator might even say prejudice—in favour of such insistent repetition of polysyllable rhyming words when they are not required by the poem's structure may at first seem unnecessary or even tautological. It took me some time to realise that the poet was as much concerned about the sound of the words and of the effect they had on the hearer as he was of their meaning.

In a poem designed to motivate and encourage self-flagellation, the full, round, rich-sounding Latin words would serve both as a stimulant to keep enthusiasts scourging themselves as well as a sort of anaesthetic to encourage them to disregard the pain the scourging caused.

This is a perspective of the poem that other translators seem to have missed or to have ignored. Their translations use words that rhyme but are often irrelevant or unsuitable, reflecting a casualness entirely at cross-purposes with the motivation of the poet.

3. The Text

Besides the rhythm and the rhyme, the other essential element of the *Stabat Mater* is the text. Judging by the acclaim the poem has enjoyed for centuries, what the poet says in it might be expected to be the most important of its three elements. It may, then, seem strange to suggest that, from one point of view, it is arguably the least important. The fact is that, once the poet has established in the opening stanza that his theme is Calvary on that first Good Friday, the rest of the narrative is already well-known.

It is only half way into the poem, when the poet asks to feel Christ's nails in his own hands and feet and to be 'intoxicated' with Christ's blood that we sit up, as it were, and pay attention to the frenetic passion of the words. This is the climax when the three elements—rhythm, rhyme and text—combine to bring it to its emotional climax.

Despite the familiarity of the narrative, the poet's genius ensures that the Latin wording of his poem is one of its most compelling features. Both metre and rhyme are combined with lush, polysyllabic words that resonate in a way that makes them both forceful and soothing at the same time. Stanza 12, where in two lines totalling nine words, four powerful words rhyme is, as I will elaborate later, an example of his forceful command of language.

As one stanza after another is sung or recited, the atmosphere created becomes progressively one of sorrow, confusion, sympathy, tragedy, suffering, empathy, repentance, immolation and, finally, hope and confidence. The rhythm drives on as if nothing could impede it and the repetitive rhyming conveys a sense of completion and finality.

And all the time as one reads the hymn, especially when it can be read out loud, one can detect in the metre a note of urgency and exigency as if this were a fleeting moment, an ephemeral opportunity that has to be taken now or may be lost for ever.

It is regrettable that these powerful qualities in the poem would escape a person who does not know Latin and whose understanding of it is derived from the more plaintive and emotional English translations. In my own translation, I have done my best to avoid this inaccurate interpretation and have concentrated on conveying an authentic representation of what I believe to be the poet's far more blunt and intense feelings.

Notes

1   F. T. Palgrave (updated by J. Press), *The Golden Treasury* (Oxford: Oxford University Press, 6th edition, 2002).
2   S. Ricks (ed), *The Oxford Book of English Verse* (Oxford: Oxford University Press, 1999).
3   A. Methuen, *An Anthology of Modern Verse* (London: Methuen & Co, 26th school edition, 1935).
4   Heman, 'Casabianca' at www.poetry-archiive.com/h/casabianca.html.
5   See Ricks, *The Oxford Book of English Verse,* poem no. 433, p. 354.
6   J. Milton, 'When I consider how my life is spent' as found in Palgrave, *The Golden Treasury*, Poem No. 70 p. 62.
7   E. A. Poe, 'The Raven' as found at www.poetry-archive.com/p/the_raven.html.
8   H. W. Longfellow, 'Hiawatha', as found at www.online-literature.com/henry_longfellow/925.
9   J. Taylor, 'Twinkle Twinkle Little Star' as found in Ricks, *The Oxford Book of English Verse*, p. 377.
10 T. Moore, 'The Vesper Bell is Stealing' as found in T. Moore, *T. Moore's Poetical Works* (London: Longman, Brown, Green and Longmans, 1843).
11 H. Leip and N. Schultze, 'Lili Marlene' first recorded by L. Anderson, 1940. See http://lyricsplayground.com/alpha/songs/l/lilimarlene.shtml.
12 For 'Won't you buy my pretty flowers?', see H. P. Danks, composer and J. Calef, lyricist, publisher Horner, J.S., Dayton, OH: 1887 as found at www.loc.gov/item/ihas.100005388/.

[13] See B. E. Bulman, *Stabat Mater* in www.warnerclassics.com/
      downloads/df/5756702.pdf. See below p. 150.
[14] See D. F. MacCarthy, 'A Translation of the Stabat Mater', in
      The Sacred Heart Review, 35/15 (7 April 1906) at
      http://newspapers.bc.edu/Boston College. See below p. 155.
[15] See E. McKenna, ed., 'Stabat Mater' in *The Collegeville Hymnal*
      (Collegeville, MN: Liturgical Press, 1990). See below p. 159.

15

THE WORK OF TRANSLATION

HE LATIN TEXT of the first stanza of the *Stabat Mater* in the *Graduale Romanum* is unforgettable.[1] In just nine words that sound like drum beats at a military funeral a mood of deepest pathos is established. The narrator is speaking as an eyewitness, recalling the scene at Calvary on that first Good Friday.

Unlike the ignorant onlookers enjoying the spectacle of three criminals being crucified, he realises the enormity of the greatest iniquity in human history. God's own creatures are killing his Son who, out of love for them, had come on earth to save them.

Christ's human mother was standing helplessly nearby suffering with him. Who could not want to share both her suffering and that of her Son in recompense for the wrongs we have done? By asking Mary to allow us to do that, would we not merit her help in winning ourselves a place in Paradise? The first stanza sets the scene.

Stanza 1

> *Stabat Mater dolorosa*
> *juxta crucem lacrimosa*
> *dum pendebat Filius*

Literal translation:

> The grieving Mother
> stood beside the cross weeping
> while her Son was hanging

In Latin, the sonorous quality of those first nine words is stunning. The regular beat and the softly rhyming polysyllable words give the three short lines a depth and strength no translation could surpass.

Even without Latin, one can experience some of the impact by reading the first line with the stresses marked as follows: STA-bat MAT-er DO-lo-RO-sa. The combination of the rhythm and the 'a' and 'o' rhyming syllables have an effect like the sound of the soldiers driving the nails into the wood of the cross through the hands and feet of Christ and the two robbers crucified with him.

My first English draft of this stanza was as follows:

Near the cross, her vigil keeping
stood the doleful Mother weeping
while her Son was hanging there

When I compared it with the popular English version by Edward Caswall that I had first seen over seventy years previously, I found his was:

At the cross her station keeping
stood the mournful Mother weeping
close to Jesus to the last

I am satisfied that my version was good from the verse point of view and was much closer to the original than Caswall's, which does not even mention Jesus on the cross. But in case I would be accused of plagiarism, I decided to drop my first and better draft and substitute the next best version I could devise which is this:

Near the cross his anguish sharing
stood the Mother near despairing
while her Son was hanging there

This is a fairly faithful translation of the Latin. In order to get two suitable words to rhyme, I had to drop the adjectives describing Mary as 'doleful' and 'tearful' and depict her as 'near despairing'. This gave me the rhyme and by adding the 'near' I avoided the theological blunder of accusing Mary of despairing.

To help the reader to compare my translation with those of the three other English translators I have studied — and whom I will introduce later — I give their versions of the first stanza as follows:

Bulman:

> Mother bowed with grief appalling
> must thou watch, with tears slow falling
> on the cross Thy dying Son

MacCarthy:

> By the cross, on which suspended
> with his bleeding hands extended
> hung that Son she so adored

Collegeville:

> At the cross her station keeping
> Mary stood in sorrow weeping
> when her Son was crucified

I have no hesitation in claiming my version is more accurate than the others and is as close to the emotional atmosphere of the Latin original as any of them.

Note:

It is worth mentioning here that Mary is described by the poet and by all the prose or poetry translations that I have read as standing at, by, next to or near the cross and some of the best-known paintings of the Crucifixion also represent her like that.

In fact, the women would probably have not been allowed too close. The centurion, knowing the hatred the Jewish people as a whole had for their Roman occupiers, would not have hesitated, if he had thought it necessary, to stick his sword or his lance into an obstreperous bystander. He would recognise that feelings were running high on the eve of that Passover Sabbath. He had seen how Pilate, the Governor of Palestine, had ordered Jesus to be viciously scourged in the hope of satisfying the crowd's blood lust that the Jewish rabbis had whipped up.

So Mary and a few others of Christ's women followers would have been huddled on one side of the hill. They would have been near enough to see what was happening to Jesus, especially after the cross had been lifted into the hole and stones piled round to keep it steady. For Mary, weeping inconsolably, wiping her tears with her veil, it would have been a special torture to be in sight of her Son and yet be unable to lift a hand to help him or even to wipe the blood and sweat off his face.

How she could stand there and not either run away or risk being killed by hastening to her Son's aid is hard to understand. It must have taken massive self-control or divine help to suffer as she did in so many ways and in such a state of helplessness.

Nowadays, a crucifixion would be regarded as a barbaric practice. In the Roman Empire they were commonplace. Only some one hundred years before Jesus' crucifixion, a Roman general called Crassus had crucified six thousand of Spartacus' slave rebels, placing their crosses at regular intervals all along both sides of the 200 kilometres of the Via Appia between Capua and Rome. It was not until 337 AD that the Emperor Constantine, after his conversion to Christianity, abolished crucifixion.

Stanza 2

> *Cuius animam gementem*
> *contristatam et dolentem*
> *pertransivit gladius*

Literal translation:

> Through whose moaning
> sad and grieving soul
> the sword penetrated

My version:

> Hers the soul so devastated
> sorrowful and desolated
> that the sword to pierce did dare

Note:

I found the first two Latin lines here a bit over-elaborate. Two 3-syllable words and one 4-syllable one, all meaning the same thing, are used to describe Mary's sorrow. The sonorous Latin and the repetitive rhyming have a dramatic and partly intimidating effect, which is clearly what the poet wanted.

Then two words, *pertransivit gladius*, meaning 'the sword penetrated right through', reproduce that powerful feeling of someone committing a violent deed with no compunction and with no possibility of being stopped.

My last line is awkward enough in English but it was the only way to get a rhyme for the last word of the previous stanza.

Stanza 3

> *O quam tristis et afflicta*
> *fuit illa benedicta*
> *Mater Unigeniti*

Literal translation:

> O how sad and afflicted
> was that blessed
> Mother of an only child

My version:

> O how sad and so dejected
> was that Mother so respected
> of her sole-begotten one

Note:

To describe Mary as 'blessed' at a time when she was watching her Son being crucified seems incongruous. I suspect the poet's choice of *benedicta* was dictated by his need of a suitable rhyme to match *afflicta*. 'Respected' was the most appropriate English equivalent I could find to rhyme with 'dejected'.

Stanza 4

> *Quae maerebat et dolebat*
> *pia Mater, dum videbat*
> *nati poenas inclyti*

Literal translation:

> the Holy Mother who mourned
> and lamented as she saw
> the torment of her illustrious offspring

My version:

> Holy Mother, tearful, doleful
> seeing all those wounds so woeful
> of her own illustrious Son

Note:

In Chapter 21, I have expanded on my views on the different English translations of this stanza and of

Stanzas 8 and 12. Here, I just note that the word 'illustrious' is another word that seems out of place in a hymn about Christ being crucified but it is a direct translation of the Latin *inclyti*. Probably another instance of the poet's difficulty in finding a rhyme, a problem that English language translators experience even more.

Stanza 5

> *Quis est homo qui non fleret*
> *Matrem Christi si videret*
> *In tanto supplicio?*

Literal translation:

> Who is the man who would not cry
> if he saw the Mother of Christ
> in such distress?

My version:

> Is there someone so uncaring
> as to shun that Mother sharing
> In that monstrous punishment?

Note:

At first reading, this stanza and the next seemed to be the easiest in the whole poem to translate while retaining the rhythm and rhyming arrangement. In fact, they proved to be the most demanding of all and I had to leave them to the last.

Gender equality demanded a change in the first line to replace 'man' with 'someone'. The key word in the rest of the stanza is *'supplicio'*, meaning 'entreaty' or 'punishment' according to what dictionary you consult. I rejected 'entreaty' on the grounds that a criminal's mother, as Mary legally was on Calvary, would get short shrift if she began pleading for mercy. The Roman centurion, even if he had the inclination, would not have had the authority to mitigate the punishment.

Stanza 6

> *Quis non posset contristari*
> *Christi Matrem contemplari*
> *dolentem cum Filio?*

Literal translation:

> Who could not sympathise
> while watching the Mother of Christ
> mourning with her Son?

My version:

> Who would fail to share the sorrow
> Son's and Mother's grief to borrow
> In their sad abandonment?

Note:

Again a very easy stanza to translate. The challenge was to find English words that not only mean the same as the Latin but also maintain the trochee metre and rhyme with one another. I spent days going through all possible alternatives and variations and finally had to end up with what appears here. I used the word 'abandonment' to recall one of Christ's final words before he died: 'My God, my God why hast thou forsaken me.'

Stanza 7:

> *Pro peccatis suae gentis*
> *vidit Jesum in tormentis*
> *et flagellis subditum*

Literal translation:

> For the sins of his people
> she saw Jesus in torments
> and subdued by the scourges.

My version:

> For the sins of his own creatures
> Mary saw his anguished features
> as the scourges took their toll

Note:

The literal translation of the first line of this stanza is 'For the sins of his people' or alternatively 'nation'. This reflects the traditional Catholic condemnation of the Jews as deicides or killers of God. Until 1989 one of the ten Solemn Intercessions in the Good Friday liturgy was for 'the perfidious Jews',[2] a description dropped in the post-Vatican II revision of the liturgy.

The wording was changed by Pope Paul VI in 1969 to read 'Let us pray for the Jewish people, the first to hear the word of God, that they may continue to grow in the love of his name and in faithfulness to his Covenant.'[3] A belated but welcome revocation of a reprehensible slur.

In translating this line, Caswall used 'For the sins of his own nation' and MacCarthy had 'For his people's sins atoning'. Bulman cleverly rendered the line as 'For the sins of every nation'. Collegeville's translation sidestepped the problem of translation by ignoring the line completely. My own choice of 'creatures' was to avoid an unfair reflection on the Jews and to express the whole human race's complicity in the Crucifixion.

Stanza 8

> *Vidit suum dulcem Natum*
> *moriendo desolatum*
> *dum emisit spiritum*

Literal translation:

> She saw her sweet child
> dying desolate
> as he released his spirit

My version:

> She beheld her Son and master
> die in desolate disaster
> as he yielded up his soul

Note:

This was a straightforward enough stanza to translate. However, no English translation could capture the sombre, echoing *–um* endings of the Latin words. In translating the second line I tried to capture the same sad, dull sound by using words starting in 'd'. *The Catholic Encyclopedia*, says that, on hearing Pergolesi's musical version of this stanza, the German poet Ludwig Tieck confessed: 'I had to turn away to hide my tears, especially at the place, *Vidit suum dulcet Natum*.'[4]

Stanza 9

> *Eia Mater, fons amoris*
> *me sentire vim doloris*
> *fac, ut tecum lugeam*

Literal translation:

> O, Mother, fount of love,
> make me feel the power of suffering
> so that I can mourn with you

My version:

Holy Mother, fount of gladness
make me feel the power of sadness
so that I may grieve with thee

Note:

At this stage of the poem, the poet, who up to now has
been sympathetic and reverent as a third party observer,
suddenly changes his approach. In this and the eight
subsequent stanzas he addresses Mary directly. He is
no longer an outsider but an active participant in the
drama. In this stanza he flares up passionately and asks
to be allowed to share Christ's suffering.

This is also where the poet seems to be crossing a
theological line by asking Mary to do something which
is beyond human powers. In an earlier chapter I have
explained why this was enough for me to rule out Pope
Innocent III as the poem's author.

I could not find any suitable rhyme for 'suffering'
so I had to substitute the word 'sadness.'

Stanza 10

Fac, ut ardeat cor meum
in amando Christum Deum
ut sibi complaceam

Literal translation:

Make my heart rejoice
in loving the Christ God
so that I may please him

My version:

Make my heart be ever burning
for the love of Christ be yearning
so may I his solace be

Note:

In this stanza, except the specified rhymes at the end of lines 1 and 2, the poet includes none of the internal rhymes he often uses. The wording is ordinary enough but the repeated 'a' sounds in *ardeat, amando* and *complaceam* add a rich and mellifluous tone.

Stanza 11

> *Sancta Mater, istud agas*
> *crucifixi fige plagas*
> *cordi meo valide*

Literal translation:

> Holy Mother, make it happen
> Fix the wounds of the crucifix
> solidly in my heart

My version:

> Holy Mother, help me duly
> in my heart the wounds fix truly
> of the One that's crucified

Note:

This stanza is another instance where the poet asks Mary to do something for him and, by extension, for all of us. As I mentioned earlier, this is an approach that is regarded by theologians as out of order since Mary's role is merely to act as intercessor. Again the Latin text is straightforward but awkward to put into English because of the difficulty in matching the metre and rhyming scheme.

Stanza 12

> *Tui Nati vulnerati*
> *tam dignati pro me pati*
> *poenas mecum divide*

Literal translation:

Your wounded Son
So worthily for me did suffer
Share his pain with me

My version:

For my sake your Son in anguish
deigned upon the cross to languish
all his pains with me divide

Note:

For those who understand Latin, this stanza is probably the most striking in the hymn. It is the climax where the three elements — rhythm, rhyme and text — combine to bring it to its emotional peak. The poet is employing his linguistic skills by using four rhyming words in a total of eight words, something that sounds artificial in English.

Even someone with no familiarity with Latin can distinguish the four *–ati* endings. Saying them out loud captures the passion and determination of the poet. He spits out the rhyming words with machine gun-like velocity. This is a fanatic at work, using words, metre and rhyme like a whip to beat his listeners or readers into awareness and action.

For days I racked my brains in a vain attempt to replicate the feat in English by writing two lines with all the four main words rhyming. Try as I might I failed completely.

It was this stanza that convinced me the hymn was written with the flagellants in mind. As they walked along the roads scourging or beating their backs, they sang hymns to keep up their spirits in the same way that soldiers in World War I sang songs like *It's a long way to Tipperary*.

The purpose of the poem now becomes clear. The Latin poet is challenging his marchers or anyone saying, singing or listening to his poem to be inspired, provoked, induced or even shamed into enduring the sufferings of Christ's Passion, to the extent of inflicting them physically on themselves. The call to self-punishment is the result the poet intended to achieve with his choice of rhythm, rhyme and text. This is the primary and fundamental message of the *Stabat Mater*.

To help them memorise the words, the composer would use rhyme as he did so generously in this stanza. The insistent repetition of the syllable–*ati* would cheer them up and help them on their way.

Stanza 13

Fac me tecum pie flere
crucifixo condolere
donec ego vixero

Literal translation:

Let me weep piously with you
and condole with the crucified one
as long as I shall live

My version:

Let me join your pious weeping
with the crucified one keeping
watch as long as I shall live

Note:

This stanza and the next presented no difficulty in translating. As usual, what proved difficult was to retain the rhythm and find the right rhymes for my version. By this stage I was tempted to coin a maxim to the effect that the easier the Latin is to understand, the more difficult it is to reproduce its meaning, metre and rhyming.

Stanza 14

Juxta crucem tecum stare
Et me tibi sociare
In planctu desidero

Literal translation:

At the cross to stay with you
And to join with you
In mourning I wish

My version:

Near the cross to stand beside you
and to share the grief inside you
that is what I want to give

Note:

This was one of the most difficult stanzas to translate because there are no suitable English words to fit the rhythm and the rhyme. The middle line in Latin translates most accurately in modern English as 'and with you to socialise'. I didn't think that would be acceptable in the context of the *Stabat Mater*.

Stanza 15

Virgo virginum praeclara
mihi iam non sis amara
fac me tecum plangere

Literal translation:

Noble Virgin of virgins
be not bitter with me
let me to weep with you

My version:

> Virgin of all virgins splendid
> with me do not feel offended
> let me weep along with you

Note:

In the Latin version of this stanza the poet asks Mary not to be bitter (*amara*) towards him. He gives no reason as to why she should be so and I believe he was just stuck for a rhyme with the last word, *praeclara*, in the preceding line. Such are the artifices of composers and translators when in need of inspiration.

Stanza 16

> *Fac, ut portem Christi mortem*
> *passionis fac consortem*
> *et plagas recolere*

Literal translation:

> Make me bear the death of Christ
> make me share his passion
> and recall his scourges

My version:

> Make me bear Christ's crucifixion
> Share with him his dereliction
> And myself his wounds renew

Note:

At this point in the poem the writer stresses what I believe to be one of his main purposes. In this stanza and the next he is instructing Mary to find ways for him to punish himself. He wants to share Christ's passion and to suffer the scourging.

Stanza 17

> Fac me plagis vulnerari
> fac me cruce inebriari
> et cruore Filii

Literal translation:

> Let me be wounded by the scourges
> let me be inebriated by the cross
> and the blood of your Son

My version:

> Make the scourges lacerate me
> make his cross inebriate me
> your Son's blood upon me lay

Note:

Here the poet identifies himself with the flagellants and other fanatics who want to punish themselves in atonement for their sins. He asks to be wounded by the scourging, to be 'intoxicated' by the cross and by the blood of Mary's Son.

So intense is he that he departs very slightly from the strict rhythm he observes otherwise. The middle line in Latin does not flow freely as there is an extra syllable between the last two words in the line. One explanation may be that this is one of the stanzas of which there is more than one version, meaning that this particular stanza may not in fact be his. However, the emotion is much more likely to be that of an itinerant rhymester plodding the Umbrian roads with the flagellants than that one of the most powerful Popes in history sitting in Rome.

Stanza 18

Flammis ne urar succensus
per te, Virgo, sim defensus
in die iudicii

Literal translation:

Lest I be burned with flames
let me be defended through you, Virgin
on the day of judgment

My version:

Lest I burn in flames rejected,
Virgin, let me be protected
through you on the Judgement Day

Note:

Now the poet, hopeful that his self-punishment has
earned him the reward, wants to be assured that Mary
will protect him from being assigned to hell on Judgement Day.

Stanza 19

Christe, cum sit hinc exire
da per Matrem me venire
ad palmam victoriae

Literal translation:

Christ, when I must go from here
grant that through your Mother I come
to the palm of victory

My version:

Christ, when hence I'm called to meet Thee
Let thy Mother come to greet me
With the palm of victory

Note:

In these last two stanzas the poet addresses Christ directly. He asks him to permit his mother to lead him to the palm of glory and that Christ himself would arrange that his soul be given the glory of Paradise.

Stanza 20

> Quando corpus morietur,
> fac, ut animae donetur
> paradisi gloria. Amen. Alleluia.

Literal translation:

> When the body will die
> Let my soul be granted
> the glory of Paradise. Amen.

My version:

> When my body is arisen
> Make my soul, all sins forgiven
> Rest in Paradise with Thee. Amen.

Note:

This was a straightforward enough stanza to translate although keeping the rhythm while finding words to rhyme was, as usual, the trouble. So instead of being given the glory of Paradise I had to be content with resting there.

I am not exaggerating when I say that some of these three line stanzas took days and even weeks to translate within the parameters I had set myself when I started.

The two biggest drawbacks were that Latin and English are dissimilar in both rhythm and rhyme, two of the most important constituents of poetry. These are especially significant in a poem like the *Stabat Mater* where the poet is using them to create in those reciting it a kind of hypnosis that would encourage them to punish themselves.

In retrospect, I think it could be argued that a prose translation would achieve that result much more easily and would be much easier to write. Free of the restrictions of the metre and the rhyming arrangement, it could possibly express the emotional effect of the original and the purpose that effect was intended to realise. And that, of course, is the function of and challenge for the translator.

Could all my work then have been unnecessary? That would be a cruel question with which to conclude. In fact, I have no hesitation in dismissing the possibility out of hand. It is precisely the rhythm and rhymes that give the Latin poem its power and majesty. The vagaries of grammar ensure that no English translation will ever be as effective as the Latin original. We translators will have to be content with being runners-up.

Notes

1   See *Graduale Romanum* (Vatican Edition, 1908) at www.ccwatershed.org/media/pdfs/13/07/11/17-23-33-0.pdf (Corpus Christi, TX: Corpus Christi Watershed, 2013).

2   The Latin word used is 'perfidies'. Some have translated this perhaps more correctly as 'faithless' or 'unbelieving', rather than 'perfidious'.

3   See *The Roman Missal* (International Commission on English in the Liturgy © ICEL 1973) (*Missale Romanum* 1969 translation).

4   See *The Catholic Encyclopedia* (New York: Robert Appleton Co., 1912), vol. XIV, p. 240. See also my notes about this stanza in Chapter 18.

16

MY NEW TRANSLATION

THIS IS MY translation of the poem that I analysed stanza by stanza in the previous chapter. Displayed without interruption as it is here, the text is easier to follow and the uninterrupted sequence of all the stanzas conveys a clearer impression of the mood of the poem.

I have already explained, perhaps *ad nauseam*, the reasons for my decision to replicate, as far as possible, the words, the metre and the rhyming format of the original, so I will not overegg the pudding here.

I have also described the difficulties in translating poetry from Latin into English and I trust that this explains why the wording in some of my stanzas is as it is. So with that I leave readers to form their own judgement about my version.

Translation by Desmond Fisher

1. Near the cross his anguish sharing
stood the Mother near despairing
while her Son was hanging there

2. Hers the soul so devastated
sorrowful and desolated
that the sword to pierce did dare

3. O how sad and so dejected
was that Mother so respected
of her sole-begotten one

4. Holy Mother, tearful, doleful,
seeing all those wounds so woeful
of her own illustrious Son

5. Is there someone so uncaring
as to shun that Mother sharing
in that monstrous punishment?

6. Who would fail to share the sorrow
Son's and Mother's grief to borrow
in their sad abandonment?

7. For the sins of his own creatures
Mary saw his anguished features
as the scourges took their toll

8. She beheld her Son and master
die in desolate disaster
as he yielded up his soul

9. Holy Mother, fount of gladness
make me feel the power of sadness
so that I may grieve with Thee

10. Make my heart be ever burning
for the love of Christ be yearning
so may I his solace be

11. Holy Mother, help me duly
in my heart the wounds fix truly
of the One that's crucified

12. For my sake your Son in anguish
deigned upon the cross to languish
all his pains with me divide

13. Let me join your pious weeping
with the crucified one keeping
watch as long as I shall live

14. Near the cross to stand beside you
and to share the grief inside you
that is what I want to give

15. Virgin of all virgins splendid
with me do not feel offended
let me weep along with you

16. Make me bear Christ's crucifixion
share with him his dereliction
and myself his wounds renew

17. Make the scourges lacerate me
make his cross inebriate me
your Son's blood upon me spray

18. Lest I burn in flames rejected,
Virgin, let me be protected
through you on the Judgement Day

19. Christ, when hence I'm called to meet Thee
let Thy Mother come to greet me
with the palm of victory

20. When my body is arisen
may my soul, all sins forgiven
rest in Paradise with Thee.

Amen. Alleluia.

17

COMPARISONS AND CONTRASTS

s SOON AS I had finished my translation of the *Stabat Mater*, I began to compare it with those of my main co-translators. I use that description rather than 'rivals' which seems too conceited since their work has already been published while mine, at the time of writing, has not. Nor will I refer to them as 'colleagues' which is unseemly, considering that three of them are dead and the fourth is an institution. I had kept to my decision not to look at these other versions until I had finished my own first draft, so I was interested to see how we compared.

On the hypothesis that Jacopone is the author, there can be no doubt that the *Stabat Mater*, and the poet's whole lifestyle after his wife's tragic death, clearly express his purpose. It is to incite in people reading or listening to his verse, feelings of outrage, of empathy and of remorse for the atrocity of Calvary. In turn, these feelings would create in them an overwhelming desire to share personally the sufferings of Christ and his mother by engaging in self-punishment and encouraging others to follow suit.

A poet's manner of putting across such ideas is to embody them in verse, using poetry's tools of language, metre and rhyme. It is, therefore, logical to start from the position that the best translations are those that most faithfully replicate the language, the meaning and, above all, the mood of the original work as conveyed by its rhythm and rhyme.

As I noted earlier, there are as many as sixty or more English translations of the *Stabat Mater*. Nearly all of them are in prose form and so of no relevance to my present purpose. I now propose to compare my own translation against each of the four most familiar English translations and the original Latin poem. Since it would be too much to do so using all twenty stanzas of each version, the texts of the earlier translations are given in the following pages and readers can match them against one another and mine. Meantime, I have selected what I consider to be the three most significant stanzas in the poem for comparison here.

These three stanzas have been chosen because they are conspicuous by the way they use words, rhythm and rhyme to convey a specific message and to create a particular mood. The criterion I will use is the measure of how close each translation comes to doing likewise, which is, of course, the purpose of translating.

How clearly, then, do these five English language translations, including my own, of the *Stabat Mater* comprehend the poet's aims and translate them into poetry? To what extent do they adopt his poetic techniques? How far do their various versions capture the mood of the original poem and how do they compare with one another? These are the questions for discussion here.

Examination of the five versions of the three stanzas considered here should help readers appreciate both the ways in which the translators faced this challenge and how successful they were in producing a result as striking as the original. The stanzas that I have chosen for this purpose are Numbers 4, 8 and 12. To start with, here are the different versions of Stanza 4.

Stanza 4 Original:

Quae maerébat et dolébat
pia Mater, dum vidébat
nati poenas ínclyti.

Literal translation:

The holy Mother who mourned and lamented
as she saw the punishment
of her illustrious offspring

Caswall:

Christ above in torment hangs
she beneath beholds the pangs
of her dying glorious Son

Bulman:

She, whose grieving was perceiving
contemplating, unabating
all the anguish of her Son

MacCarthy:

Oh, the grieving, sense–bereaving
of her heaving breast, perceiving
the dread sufferings of her Son

Collegeville:

Ever-patient in her yearning
though her tear-filled eyes were burning
Mary gazed upon her Son

My version:

Holy Mother, tearful, doleful
seeing all those wounds so woeful
of her own illustrious Son

Except for my own, these renderings are not translations of the original text. They resemble it only to the extent that both Latin and English versions use a string of rhyming words to generate an emotional reaction to the events they are describing. The difference between them is in the way the words they choose portray Mary's emotional feelings at Calvary, a key element of the poem.

The poet's use of his language's softly rhyming suffixes (*maerebat, dolebat* and *videbat*), especially when the first two of them mean the same thing, slows down the pace of the metre to that of a tired band of flagellants marching up and down the winding Umbrian roads. The effect is to interpret Mary's reaction to the barbarity of Calvary as a despairing but yet resigned acceptance of the will of an omniscient and omnipotent God. That is what the poet intends and it is in accord with his religious convictions.

The English translators, by comparison much poorer in words that both rhyme and mean the same, have to compromise to an extent that creates a totally different effect. Wanting to replicate the impact of the repeated rhyming and short of suitable words to do so, they add in words that do rhyme but have no relevance to the text they are translating. The result is to speed up the pace of the verse to a degree unwarranted by the original wording. It also gives a picture of the events on Calvary on that first Good Friday that is markedly at odds with the poet's portrayal.

The original forthright Latin wording indicates that the poet decided first what he wanted to say and then found rhyming words to express it. For their part, the Bulman, MacCarthy and Collegeville versions, in a variation of putting the cart before the horse, seem first to have selected the rhyming words and then used any phrases that came to mind to fill out the lines, regardless of their relevance to the original text.

Another stanza in the poem where the poet of the *Stabat Mater* shows off the advantages his language has over ours is Stanza 8. The cold fact is that Latin, by virtue of its structure, can provide a greater choice of sonorous and emotive words than English. Even if they are not being used for rhyme, the very sound of them can produce an emotional response that does not need comprehension of the words to experience.

Stanza 8 Original:

Vidit suum dulcem Natum
moriéndo desolátum
dum emísit spíritum

Literal translation:

She saw her sweet Child
dying desolate
as he released his spirit

Read aloud, the Latin words sound protective and poignant as Mary sees her dear son dying in desolation. The picture they create is of Christ's dead body slumped down over the cross as the crowds go back into the city and dusk begins to cloud the hill of Calvary. Only the men remain to take down the limp body and place it in her lap to clean and smear with myrrh and aloes before he is wrapped in a shroud and laid in the cave.

It is more difficult to achieve the same effect in English. Caswall misplaced his stanzas but his corresponding Stanza 7 reads:

> Bruised, derided, cursed, defiled
> she beheld her tender Child
> all with scourges rent

Bulman's version of the stanza is:

> Saw her Jesus foully taken
> languishing, by all forsaken,
> when his spirit passed away

MacCarthy's version is:

> Saw her loved one, her consoler
> dying in his dreadful dolour
> till at length his spirit fled

Collegeville's corresponding stanza 7 reads:

> Christ she saw with life-blood failing
> all her anguish unavailing
> saw him breathe his very last

My own version of a stanza that I found particularly difficult is:

> She beheld her Son and master
> die in desolate disaster
> as he yielded up his soul

My first observation was that none of my four fellow translators adopted all the constraints I had placed on myself. Only one of the four maintains the original metre from start to finish. Some partly ignore the rhyming formula. All, to varying degrees, disregard the text and invent whole stanzas that have little or no resemblance to the original. I believe I have been more rigorous than the others in doing justice to the poet's example in all respects.

However, I don't think any of these English versions of the stanza is outstanding though mine is the closest to the original text. They all seem to lack the desolation and solemnity of the Latin original. But, given the kind of job to be done and the tools to do it with, they were probably the best that could be expected.

The simple truth is that inflected Latin words, trailing softly rhyming suffixes, sound far more welcoming and soothing than their English equivalents.

To give them their due, however, the four other translators were at least making some attempt to translate the words of that particular stanza. However, more often than not, whether defeated by the difficulty of the challenge or carried away by the emotion of the original poet, they simply do not bother. Instead, they seem to ignore the rules and conventions of orthodox translation.

A good instance of this can be found in Stanza 12. It was that which convinced me the hymn was written with the flagellants in mind. Fourteenth century peasant marchers, singing a lengthy song in a semi-foreign language as Latin would be to villagers speaking the Umbrian dialect, needed some sort of incentive. Whether they were flagellants or not, they had to keep moving and they had to remember the words.

The rapidly repeated rhyming words of the *Stabat Mater*, hammered out in quick succession, would help to reinvigorate them as they trudged along in the hot sun. The effect would be to restore their confidence in the merit of what they were doing, revive their vigour and strengthen their resolve to keep going, however exhausted they felt.

The explosion of rhymes would also act as a reminder of where they were in the song. In Jacopone da Todi's lifetime, there were no hymn books or hymn sheets to remind them of the words of the next line or the next stanza. The marchers had to rely on their memories and occasional jolts acted like signposts to show what part of the poem was coming next. A useful mnemonic would both encourage them to keep moving, as well as help them remember the words of the hymn. So the poet of the *Stabat Mater* may have used a few tricks of the trade to help them.

Stanza 12 is where I feel the Latin poet was doing just that. He had a clear justification—a halfway jolt to reinvigorate the marchers and to refresh their memories. Bulman and MacCarthy had no such rationale. They seem to be doing it merely to impress and to obscure the fact that what they are writing is their own invention, not translation. As I have already noted, this runs the risk of unfairly distorting a non-Latin speaker's impression of the original text. But let the different narratives speak for themselves.

Stanza 12 Original :

> *Tui Nati vulneráti,*
> *tam dignáti pro me pati*
> *poenas mecum dívide*

A literal translation is:

> Divide with me the pains
> your wounded Son suffered
> so worthily for me

As an example of what I mean, this stanza is probably, for a listener or a translator, the most arresting in the hymn from a technical point of view. The poet, intentionally or not, displays his poetic skills by using four rhyming words that make perfect sense in a total of eight words, something nearly impossible in English.

Even someone unfamiliar with Latin can distinguish the four *–ati* endings in this stanza. Saying them out loud intensifies the passion and tenacity of the poem and reveals the poet's deepest emotions. This is a fanatic at work, using the insistent rhyme like a whip to urge the marchers on and beat them into a mood of remorse and repentance.

For days I racked my brains in a vain attempt to replicate the feat in English. The challenge was to write two lines of four trochees that faithfully translate the original text and in which every second stressed syllable rhymes. Try as I might I failed completely. The two languages, Latin and English, which I had always believed were very similar in many ways, proved to be much more different than I had realised. Therefore translating one to the other became much more difficult than I had anticipated. I am sure many linguists and translators have found that out, but it was a new and chastening experience for me.

To give them their due, two of my fellow-translators, Bulman and MacCarthy, succeeded spectacularly in finding the rhyme though at the cost of abandoning any pretence of keeping to the original words. Bulman's version of that stanza is almost hysterical in its wording. The meaning of the words is both incoherent and irrelevant and the effect produced is one of chaos and pandemonium. She writes:

> Hate, misprision, scorn, derision
> thirst assailing, failing vision
> railing, ailing, deal to me

The only resemblance that this translation bears to the original is in its extravagant intensity.

MacCarthy's version of the same stanza is not quite as hectic but here again the meaning of the words is subordinate to the rhyme and the rhythm. He writes:

Ever leading where thy bleeding
Son is pleading for my needing
let me in his wounds take part

I select these two versions to illustrate one of the main
points I have been emphasising. This is that, regardless
of the meaning of the words, both rhythm and rhyme
are able to create an emotional reaction, thus enabling
a poet to influence, even manipulate, the reaction of
his readers or reciters.

My assessment is that Bulman's and MacCarthy's
translations illustrate this precise point and many
readers may welcome their versions. However, both
seem to me to do an injustice to the Latin poet by
falsely interpreting his words rather than honestly
trying to translate them.

Caswall's version, like my own, is a much more
genuine translation of the original but his elision of the
unstressed syllable at the end of the first two lines in
the stanza and the absence of internal rhyme make it
less exciting. His reads:

Let me share with thee His pain
who for all my sins was slain
who for me in torments died

The Collegeville version of this stanza is a good
example of the sloppy, oversweet tone of the institution's whole translation. It reads:

Fairest maid of all creation
Queen of hope and consolation
let me feel your grief sublime

My own version, closer to Caswall's than any of the
others, is:

> For my sake your Son in anguish
> deigned upon the cross to languish
> all his pains with me divide

This is much closer to the original in meaning and in mood and therefore in its effect on a hearer or reader. This judgment is not simply a matter of taste or of being finicky or pedantic. After spending nearly six months on translating sixty short lines, I realise how difficult it is to translate from Latin to English while faithfully observing metric and rhyming patterns, neither of which suit the English language. And even allowing that the poet of the *Stabat Mater* may have been less interested in the exact meaning of his words than in the sound they made in Latin, there are limits to the degree to which a translator can ignore them.

All four of the English translations that preceded my own are to be found in the following pages and I invite readers to compare them with mine and come to their own conclusions about which they like best.

18

THE ORIGINAL *STABAT MATER*

 HE FOLLOWING IS the official version of the *Stabat Mater*, as approved by the Roman Catholic Church and used in the *Graduale Romanum*.[1] Several other versions of what is claimed to be the original Latin text exist. They differ slightly from this version or have some additional stanzas but this is the version that Catholics now use.

As I have sought to establish in this book, its most likely author is Jacopone da Todi, whose real name was Jacopo Benedicti or Benedetti.

The poem was written about AD 1286 in the ecclesiastical Latin that had replaced classical Latin around the end of the fifth century AD. This was the *lingua franca* of cultured circles throughout most of Europe from then until comparatively recent times. It still plays a part in medicine and law.

The Latin used by the educated upper-class people during the lifetime of Christ would be classical Latin. At that time, the alphabet had only twenty-three letters, with W, U, and J being later additions. This would mean, for instance, that the Latin version of the sign in three languages, (Hebrew, Greek and Latin), that Pilate wrote and ordered to be nailed to Christ's Cross (John 19: 19–20) would have read *IESVS NAZARENVS REX IVDAEORVM*. However, I have chosen the alphabet that the thirteenth century poet of the *Stabat Mater* would have used and not that of the time he writes about.

Gregorian chant versions of the poem were later adopted by the Franciscan friars and soon spread around Europe. Other hymns like it were also introduced as sequences into the liturgy until they became so numerous (over 4,500) that all were banned by the sixteenth century Council of Trent except for four—*Victimae paschalis laudes, Veni sancte spiritus, Lauda Sion* and the *Dies Irae.*

In 1727, Pope Benedict XIII reinstated the *Stabat Mater* to the liturgy and in 1913, Pope Pius X assigned it to the feast of Sorrows of the Blessed Virgin Mary on 15 September. In some churches it is sung during the Stations of the Cross service during Lent.

In Latin the stress is usually on the first syllable of a two-syllable word and on the strongest syllable in longer words. In the text below I have marked the stressed syllables with an acute accent.

1. Stabat Mater dolorósa
Juxta crucem lacrimósa,
Dum pendébat Filius.

2. Cuius ánimam geméntem,
Contristátam et doléntem,
Pertransívit gládius.

3. O quam tristis et afflícta
Fuit illa benedícta
Mater Unigéniti!

4. Quae maerébat et dolébat
Pia Mater, dum vidébat
Nati poenas ínclyti.

5. Quis est homo qui non fleret,
Matrem Christi si vidéret
In tanto supplício?

6. *Quis non posset contristári,*
Christi Matrem contemplári
Dólentem cum Fílio?

7. *Pro peccátis suae gentis*
Vidit Jesum in torméntis,
Et flagéllis súbditum.

8. *Vidit suum dulcem Natum*
Moriéndo desolátum,
Dum emísit spíritum.

9. *Eia, Mater, fons amóris,*
Me sentíre vim dolóris
Fac, ut tecum lúgeam.

10. *Fac, ut árdeat cor meum*
In amándo Christum Deum,
Ut sibi compláceam.

11. *Sancta Mater, istud agas,*
Crucifíxi fige plagas
Cordi meo válide.

12 *Tui Nati vulneráti,*
Tam dignáti pro me pati,
Poenas mecum dívide.

13. *Fac me tecum pie flere,*
Crucifíxo condoláre,
Donec ego vixero.

14. *Juxta Crucem tecum stare,*
Et me tibi sociáre
In planctu desídero.

15. *Virgo vírginum praeclára,*
Mihi jam non sis amára:
Fac me tecum plángere.

16. *Fac, ut portem Christi mortem,*
Passiónis fac consórtem,
Et plagas recólere.

17. Fac me plagis vulnerári,
Fac me Cruce inebriári,
Et cruóre Fílii.

18. Flammis ne urar succénsus,
Per te, Virgo, sim defénsus
In die judícii.

19. Christe, cum sit hinc exíre,
Da per Matrem me veníre
Ad palmam victóriae.

20. Quando corpus moriétur,
Fac, ut ánimae donétur
Paradísi glória.
Amen. Allelúia.

Notes

[1] See *Graduale Romanum* (Vatican Edition, 1908) at
www.ccwatershed.org/media/pdfs/13/07/11/17-23-33-0.pdf
(Corpus Christi, TX: Corpus Christi Watershed, 2013).

19

TRANSLATION BY
EDWARD CASWALL

UDGING BY ITS consistent use in religious publications for the past century and, in more recent years, on the Internet, Edward Caswall's version is, up to now, the best-known English language translation of the *Stabat Mater*.[1] It is the one that usually accompanies the original Latin in any Internet search for the poem. It is the one I first encountered seventy-six years ago and greatly admired. Now that I have followed in Caswall's tracks, I am rather more critical.

Caswall (or Caswell) (1814–1878) was born in Hampshire and educated at Oxford. Like his father and brother he became an Anglican vicar and later converted to Catholicism. Eventually he was ordained a priest and translated many hymns and other religious writings from Latin to English.

His 1849 text is fairly true to the original throughout though he ignores the original texts of Stanza 4 and 12 and transposes parts of Stanzas 7 and 8. In places, some will find the prose too saccharine and sentimental with words like whelmed, swooned and hence, giving it a dated and artificial flavour. This is especially so when he is endeavouring to show sympathy with the grieving mother and it risks making his expression of sorrow unconvincing.

Apart from this, Caswall makes a real effort to be true to the original text though his wording, like that of my own version, has a slightly stilted, unnatural quality that is probably inevitable in the circumstances.

I was, however, disenchanted to discover that the translator I had most admired when I first came across the *Stabat Mater* had broken one of the main rules I had thought sacrosanct to translators. He had failed to maintain the poem's original trochaic metre, holding it only for the first two stanzas and the eighth.

Presumably finding it too difficult, he changes into a far less demanding metre for the other seventeen stanzas. This involves reducing the first two lines of each stanza from eight syllables to seven so that all three lines of each stanza are the same length. In my opinion, this is more than just a technical confidence trick. Discarding the eighth syllable weakens the vigour and assertiveness of the original poem and impairs a version that is otherwise generally acceptable.

Otherwise his meticulous adherence to the original rhyming is admirable and proves that it is possible, though in my own experience very difficult, to find the most suitable English words for that purpose. All in all, this is an excellent translation that merits the widespread media attention it has been receiving for as long as I can remember. This is it:

Stabat Mater: *Translated by Edward Caswall*

1. At the Cross her station keeping,
stood the mournful Mother weeping,
close to Jesus to the last:

2. Through her heart, His sorrow sharing,
all His bitter anguish bearing,
now at length the sword had passed.

3. Oh how sad and sore distressed
was that Mother, highly blest
of the sole-begotten One!

4. Christ above in torment hangs;
she beneath beholds the pangs
of her dying glorious Son.

5. Is there one who would not weep
whelmed in miseries so deep
Christ's dear Mother to behold?

6. Can the human heart refrain
from partaking in her pain,
in that Mother's pain untold?

7. Bruised, derided, cursed, defiled,
she beheld her tender Child:
All with bloody scourges rent.

8. For the sins of His own nation
saw Him hang in desolation,
Till His spirit forth He sent.

9. O thou Mother! fount of love!
Touch my spirit from above;
make my heart with thine accord:

10. Make me feel as thou hast felt;
make my soul to glow and melt
with the love of Christ my Lord.

11. Holy Mother! pierce me through;
in my heart each wound renew
of my Saviour crucified:

12. Let me share with thee His pain,
who for all my sins was slain,
who for me in torments died.

13. Let me mingle tears with thee,
mourning Him who mourned for me,
all the days that I may live:

14. By the Cross with thee to stay;
there with thee to weep and pray;
is all I ask of thee to give.

15. Virgin of all virgins best!
Listen to my fond request:
let me share thy grief divine;

16. Let me, to my latest breath,
in my body bear the death
of that dying Son of thine.

17. Wounded with His every wound,
steep my soul till it hath swooned
in His very Blood away;

18. Be to me, O Virgin, nigh,
lest in flames I burn and die,
in His awful Judgment Day.

19. Christ, when Thou shalt call me hence,
by Thy Mother my defence,
by Thy Cross my victory;

20. While my body here decays,
may my soul Thy goodness praise,
safe in Paradise with Thee.

Notes

[1]   See E. Caswall, *Stabat Mater* in *Lyra Catholica* (New York: E.
Dunigan & Brother, 1851 pp. 182–186 in https://archive.org/
stream/lyracatholicacon00newy#page/n5/mode/2up.

20

TRANSLATION BY BEATRICE E. BULMAN

HE SECOND MOST frequently encountered English version of the *Stabat Mater* is that of Beatrice E. Bulman, who was born in Ramsgate in Kent in 1870 and died in Wandsworth, London, in 1950.[1] Her translation of the poem succeeds from her first line in gripping attention though it is far from being accurate. Where the Latin poet confines himself to the simple statement that the sorrowing mother stood, she paints the vivid picture of the 'Mother bowed with grief appalling.'

This is a narrative style that will appeal to some readers who will like its speed and vivacity. Almost certainly, it will displease others, especially those who understand Latin and know that, for the most part, her verses bear only limited resemblance to the equivalent text in the original. Indeed, several of her stanzas are impossible to relate to the corresponding Latin one. Only in Stanzas 9 to 11, does she adopt a softer and more restrained tone. Then, for two more stanzas and in what is almost a parody of the poet, she indulges herself in a reckless flow of rhyming words that makes no sense.

However, this style does help her to capture the vitality rather than the occasional rawness of the original poem and may therefore appeal more to some readers, especially those who might demur at the idea of self-flagellation.

She could be forgiven for expecting her readers to accept words like oppresséd, ever-blesséd and inspiréd. But a perfectionist would quibble at the demotion of 'heaven' to 'heav'n', even though this would probably go unnoticed in English poetry and would certainly be acceptable in ordinary speech.

However, her compliance with both the metre and the rhyming scheme of the original is commendable. Throughout she maintains the strict rhythm of the original trochaic metre except for a few relatively minor instances.

Her translation, which is given here, has been used as the score for many musical versions, including well-known ones by Pergolesi and Bach.

Stabat Mater: *Translated by Beatrice E. Bulman*

1. Mother bowed with grief appalling
must thou watch, with tears slow falling,
on the cross Thy dying Son!

2. Through my heart, thus sorrow riven,
must that cruel sword be driven,
as foretold—O Holy One!

3. Oh, how mournful and oppresséd
was that Mother ever-blesséd,
Mother of the Spotless One:

4. She, whose grieving was perceiving,
contemplating, unabating,
all the anguish of her Son!

5. Is there any, tears withholding,
Christ's dear Mother thus beholding,
in woe—like no other woe!

6. Who that would not grief be feeling
for that Holy Mother kneeling—
what suffering was ever so?

7. For the sins of every nation
she beheld his tribulation,
given to scourgers for a prey:

8. Saw her Jesus foully taken,
languishing, by all forsaken,
when his spirit passed away.

9. Love's sweet fountain, Mother tender,
haste this hard heart, soft to render,
make me sharer in Thy pain.

10. Fire me now with zeal so glowing,
love so rich to Jesus, flowing,
that I favour may obtain.

11. Holy Mother, I implore Thee.
crucify this heart before Thee—
guilty it is verily!

12. Hate, misprision, scorn, derision,
thirst assailing, failing vision,
railing, ailing, deal to me.

13. In Thy keeping, watching, weeping,
by the cross may I unsleeping
live and sorrow for his sake.

14. Close to Jesus, with Thee kneeling,
all Thy dolours with Thee feeling,
oh grant this—the prayer I make.

15. Maid immaculate, excelling,
peerless one, in heav'ns high dwelling,
make me truly mourn with Thee.

16. Make me sighing hear Him dying,
ever newly vivifying
the anguish He bore for me.

17. With the same scar lacerated,
by the cross enfired, elated,
wrought by love to ecstasy!

18. Thus inspiréd and affected
let me, Virgin, be protected
when sounds forth the call for me!

19. May His sacred cross defend me,
He who died there so befriend me,
that His pardon shall suffice.

20. When this earthly frame is riven,
grant that to my soul is given
all the joys of Paradise!

Notes

[1]   B. E. Bulman, *Stabat Mater* at www.warnerclassics.com/
downloads/df/5756702.pdf.

21

TRANSLATION BY
D. F. MACCARTHY

VERSION THAT APPEALS to me is that by the nineteenth century Irish poet and dramatist, Denis Florence MacCarthy (1817–1882).[1] Born in Dublin, he spent some years in the national seminary at Maynooth where he was greatly influenced by an elderly priest who was an expert on Spanish literature. This resulted in his own best work, a translation of the work of the seventeenth century Spanish dramatist, Pedro Calderón de la Barca, for which he was awarded a Royal Spanish Academy medal.

A fervent Irish nationalist, he used his talents as a poet and writer to contribute to many of the anti-British publications in the second half of the nineteenth century. My partiality for him is undoubtedly influenced by the fact that he wrote under the pseudonym 'Desmond', my own Christian name.

MacCarthy's version of the *Stabat Mater* is a literary *tour de force*. His skilful choice of language gives his version an elegance and lightness as well as a flamboyant sweep that will make an initial appeal to many readers and listeners. After a while, however, and especially for readers who know Latin, this may eventually contrast uncomfortably with the sombre mood which, except for Stanza 12, hangs over the Latin poem like a funeral pall. As a result, his audience might find his subsequent expressions of sympathy, however elegantly expressed, to be somewhat artificial and unconvincing.

The latitude in translating that MacCarthy exploits also allows him to match the original poet's adroit use of repetition to intensify the pace and drive home his message. In Stanza 12 the original author bombards the listener with two lines in which four words out of the eight in it rhyme. MacCarthy achieves the same dramatic effect, a much more difficult feat in English than in Latin, in two stanzas in his translation.

His text, like Bulman's, often bears no resemblance to the original Latin words though it catches its mood of urgency and impulsive abandon the original poet wished to convey. But instead of choosing the English word that would convey the serious intent of the Latin, they both adopt a false piety that risks becoming the poetic equivalent of purple prose.

Where he scores highly is in his staunch adherence to the original metre and rhyming arrangement. Only once, in the very last line — 'Ope in heaven its raptured eyes' — does he need to shorten one word to hold to the metre.

He also succeeds in matching or even surpassing the Latin poet's skill in finding additional internal rhymes (see his versions of Stanzas 4, 12, 13 and 16) even if he does it at the cost of abandoning all pretence of a faithful translation of the poem.

Nevertheless the confident emotional sweep of his and Bulman's versions are closer to the stark urgency of the original than the austere Caswall translation though whether either produces the emotional reaction the Latin poet sought is a moot point.

Stabat Mater: *Translated by D. F. MacCarthy*

1. By the cross, on which suspended,
With His bleeding hands extended,
Hung that Son she so adored,

2. Stood the mournful Mother weeping,
She, whose heart, its silence keeping,
Grief had cleft as with a sword.

3. Oh, that Mother's sad affliction—
Mother of all benediction—
Of the sole–begotten One;

4. Oh, the grieving, sense–bereaving,
Of her heaving breast, perceiving
The dread sufferings of her Son.

5. What man is there so unfeeling,
Who, his heart to pity steeling,
Could behold that sight unmoved?

6. Could Christ's Mother see there weeping,
See the pious Mother keeping
Vigil by the Son she loved?

7. For His people's sins atoning,
She saw Jesus writhing, groaning,
'Neath the scourge wherewith he bled:

8. Saw her loved One, her consoler,
Dying in His dreadful dolour,
Till at length His spirit fled.

9. O thou Mother of election,
Fountain of all pure affection,
Make thy grief, thy pain, my own;

10. Make my heart to God returning,
In the love of Jesus burning,
Feel the fire that thine has known.

11. Blessed Mother of prediction,
Stamp the marks of crucifixion
Deeply on my stony heart,

12. Ever leading where thy bleeding
Son is pleading for my needing,
Let me in His wounds take part.

13. Make me truly, each day newly
While life lasts, O Mother, duly
Weep with Him, the Crucified.

14. Let me, 'tis my sole demanding,
Near the cross, where thou art standing,
Stand in sorrow at thy side.

15. Queen of virgins, best and dearest,
Grant, oh, grant the prayer thou hearest,
Let me ever mourn with thee;

16. Let compassion me so fashion
That Christ's wounds, His death and passion,
Be each day renewed in me.

17. Oh, those wounds, do not deny me;
On that cross, oh, crucify me;
Let me drink His blood, I pray:

18. Then on fire, enkindled, daring,
I may stand without despairing
On that dreadful judgment-day.

19. May that cross be my salvation;
Make Christ's death my preservation;
May His grace my heart make wise;

20. And when death my body taketh,
May my soul when it awaketh
Ope in heaven its raptured eyes.

Notes

[1]   See D. F. MacCarthy, 'A Translation of the Stabat Mater', in
      The Sacred Heart Review, 35/15 (7 April 1906) at
      http://newspapers.bc.edu/Boston College.

22

TRANSLATION BY COLLEGEVILLE HYMNAL

T HE FOURTH OF the English language translations with which I compare my own is the Collegeville Hymnal version, published in 1990 by Liturgical Press, Collegeville, Minnesota.[1] The company's general editor at the time was a Chicago priest, Fr Edward McKenna. According to himself, he had previously written an English translation of the *Stabat Mater* but it was not accepted for the Hymnal.

Like myself, he was an advocate of the reforms agreed by the Second Vatican Council and, for that reason alone, I would like to have been justified in praising the Hymnal's version of the poem as beyond reproach. However, while it has many good points, it does not meet the specifications I had determined were required for it to be regarded as a faithful rendition of the original poem.

The translation was done by a Fr Roger Schoenbechler, OSB, who died in 1986. In the early stanzas, the text is reasonably faithful to the original and the metre and rhyming arrangement are adhered to. In later stanzas, however, scant attention is paid to the convention that the target or host language replicates the meaning of the words in the source language. Many of the words and even full stanzas of the original poem are ignored or substituted by material that bears little or no relevance to the Latin version.

The treatment of the original metre and rhyming arrangement is equally arbitrary. For the greatest part of the poem the trochaic tetrameter metre is faithfully observed. However, in five stanzas (15, 16, 17, 18 and 20) the metre is abandoned by the dropping of the unstressed syllable at the end of lines 1 and 2, a move that, to my mind, eliminates the intense onward drive of the original.

The same cavalier attitude is adopted for the rhyme at the end of line three on each pair of consecutive stanzas. Only in three places is it attempted, two of them by the expedient of using the same word twice and the other one properly on the very last pair of stanzas.

To some extent, the Collegeville version compensates for these technical deficiencies by reflecting the softer atmosphere of the early part of the Latin poem when the poet acts as a sympathetic observer of the scene on Calvary.

However, it fails to recognise the abrupt change in attitude in Stanza 7. At this point, the observer realises the enormity of the injustice of what is happening. No longer a passive onlooker, he is transformed into a shocked and scathing critic of what he now sees is a sacrilege—human creatures crucifying the son of their divine Creator.

From then on, the rest of the poem, except for the final three stanzas, is a strident confrontation with Mary. The compassionate observer and caustic critic is now a passionate activist, demanding Mary's intervention on his behalf so that he can share in her and her son's suffering.

To fail to reflect this aspect of the poet's gradual transformation is a weakness in this translation. To my way of thinking, rather than calling it a translation, this version, could best be described as 'based on the original' or 'an adaptation'.

To be fair, the omission of the passionate mood of a significant part of the Latin poem is, to one degree or another, a fault in all the translations that I am comparing here, including my own. Its absence dilutes or, as in the present version, altogether conceals the part the flagellant frenzy played in the whole story of the *Stabat Mater* poem. Again, readers can judge for themselves by reading the different translations.

Stabat Mater: *Collegeville Hymnal Version*

1. At the cross her station keeping
Mary stood in sorrow weeping
When her Son was crucified.

2. While she waited in her anguish,
Seeing Christ in torment languish,
Bitter sorrow pierced her heart.

3. With what pain and desolation,
With what noble resignation,
Mary watched her dying Son.

4. Ever-patient in her yearning
Though her tear-filled eyes were burning,
Mary gazed upon her Son.

5. Who, that sorrow contemplating,
On that passion meditating,
Would not share the Virgin's grief?

6. Christ she saw, for our salvation,
Scourged with cruel acclamation,
Bruised and beaten by the rod.

7. Christ she saw with life-blood failing,
All her anguish unavailing,
Saw him breathe his very last.

8. Mary, fount of love's devotion,
Let me share with true emotion
All the sorrow you endured.

9. Virgin, ever interceding,
Hear me in my fervent pleading:
Fire me with your love of Christ.

10. Mother, may this prayer be granted:
That Christ's love may be implanted
In the depths of my poor soul.

11. At the cross, your sorrow sharing,
All your grief and torment bearing,
Let me stand and mourn with you.

12. Fairest maid of all creation,
Queen of hope and consolation,
Let me feel your grief sublime.

13. Virgin, in your love befriend me,
At the Judgment Day defend me.
Help me by your constant prayer.

14. Savior, when my life shall leave me,
Through your mother's prayers receive me
With the fruits of victory.

15. Virgin of all virgins blest!
Listen to my fond request:
Let me share your grief divine.

16. Let me, to my latest breath,
In my body bear the death
Of your dying Son divine.

17. Wounded with His every wound,
Steep my soul till it has swooned
In His very blood away.

18. Be to me, O Virgin, nigh,
Lest in flames I burn and die,
In His awe-full judgment day.

19. Savior, when my life shall leave me,
Through your mother's prayers receive me,
With the fruits of victory.

20. While my body here decays
May my soul your goodness praise,
Safe in heaven eternally. Amen. Alleluia.

Notes

1   See R. Schoenbechler, 'Stabat Mater' in E. McKenna, ed., *The Collegeville Hymnal* (Collegeville, MN: Liturgical Press, 1990).

23

A Dutch Contribution

OR ANYONE INTERESTED in further information about the *Stabat Mater*, my research turned up an interesting Internet site called, with some justification, The Ultimate Stabat Mater Website. It is the creation of a Dutchman called Hans van der Velden, who died in December 2005.[1]

Now administered by his partner, Hannie van Osnabrugge, the site lists 241 different *Stabat Mater* musical versions and includes information on the composers, the music and the texts with translations in twenty-four languages. Among them are such well-known composers as Bach, Dvořák, Haydn, Kodály, Liszt, Pergolesi, Rossini, and Vivaldi.

This site is truly a work of love especially since the late Mr van der Velden described himself as an 'analphabet' or a person illiterate in musical theory and not even able to read music. Nevertheless he lists the length of the running time of each of the musical versions of the *Stabat Mater* of which he had a CD. They run from 2.04 minutes for the version of a Charles Haenni to the 88.40 minutes for Dvořák's version. The oldest version listed (1409 AD) is that of an Englishman with the iconic name of John Browne; the most recent that of a Marc Eychenne in 2008. As my own competence in music is as limited as Mr van der Velden's was, I did not stray further into this area in my research.

This site also confirms that the *Stabat Mater* was first sung by ordinary people, especially groups like the extremist bands of the *Flagellanti* and the *Bianchi* that I have described earlier. Mr van der Velden also maintains that each two consecutive stanzas had a different melody and, before printing was invented, variation of the rhyming arrangement was liberally used to help in memorising the words.

Several versions of what is claimed to be the original text exist, inevitable when different scribes were copying it. Mr van der Velden lists two slightly different 'official' versions. He also believes some parts of the version used today in Catholic churches are not from the original.

As I also did before discovering his site, he notices that the second line in Stanza 17 of the original Latin poem, if pronounced precisely, has one syllable more than the eight syllables that are otherwise routine for this poem. In addition, he notes that the last words (*victoriae, gloria*) of Stanzas 19 and 20 do not rhyme as accurately as corresponding words do elsewhere throughout the poem.

Stabat Mater: *Hans van der Velden's literal translation*

1. The grieving Mother stood
weeping beside the cross
where her Son was hanging

2. Through her weeping soul,
compassionate and grieving,
a sword passed.

3. O how sad and afflicted
was that blessed
Mother of the Only-begotten!

4. Who mourned and grieved
and trembled looking
at the torment of her glorious Child

5. Who is the person who would not weep
seeing the Mother of Christ
in such agony?

6. Who would not be able to feel compassion
on beholding Christ's Mother
suffering with her Son?

7. For the sins of his people
she saw Jesus in torment
and subjected to the scourge.

8. She saw her sweet offspring
dying, forsaken,
while He gave up His spirit

9. O Mother, fountain of love,
make me feel the power of sorrow,
that I may grieve with you

10. Grant that my heart may burn
in the love of Christ my Lord,
that I may greatly please Him

11 Holy Mother, grant
that the wounds of the Crucified
drive deep into my heart.

12. That of your wounded Son,
who so deigned to suffer for me,
I may share the pain

13. Let me sincerely weep with you,
bemoan the Crucified,
for as long as I live

14. To stand beside the cross with you,
and gladly share the weeping,
this I desire.

15. Chosen Virgin of virgins,
be not bitter with me,
let me weep with thee

16. Grant that I may bear the death of Christ,
the fate of his Passion,
and commemorate His wounds

17. Let me be wounded with His wounds,
inebriated by the cross
because of love for the Son

18. Inflame and set on fire,
may I be defended by you, Virgin,
on the day of judgement

19. Let me be guarded by the cross,
armed by Christ's death
and His grace cherish me

20. When my body dies,
grant that to my soul is given
the glory of paradise. Amen

Notes

[1]   See www.stabatmater.info.

24

THE OTHER *STABAT MATER*

OME READERS, ESPECIALLY those who are proficient in searching the Internet, may have come across another poem with several remarkable likenesses to the *Stabat Mater Dolorosa*, as well as many intrinsic differences from it. Called the *Stabat Mater Speciosa* (Stood the Beautiful Mother), its authorship has been questioned, especially recently, as much as has that of the *Dolorosa*.

The earliest mention of the *Speciosa* is in an edition of Jacopone's poems published in Brescia in 1495, nearly two hundred years after his death.[1] Both the *Dolorosa* and *Speciosa* poems are listed as his. However, in a similar collection published in Florence five years earlier and regarded by experts as a more reliable record, only the *Dolorosa* is attributed to him.

In the following centuries, the *Speciosa* was more or less ignored and it was not until comparatively recently that the question of its authorship was revived. This was undoubtedly one of outcomes of the Oxford Movement of the mid-nineteenth century that saw many so-called High Church Anglicans, mainly upper class academics—hence the 'Oxford' tag—move closer to Catholicism.

Besides seeking to bring the Catholic, Protestant and Orthodox Churches closer together, the more *avant-garde* wing of the movement encouraged Anglicanism to adapt or adopt some Catholic liturgical practices. It favoured a 'softer' form of worship, one aspect of which was a more positive acceptance of the role that Mary plays in the divine plan for redemption.

The move towards Catholicism, encouraged by personages such as John Henry Newman and Henry Edward Manning, who both subsequently became Catholic priests and later Cardinals, helped to revive interest in the *Stabat Mater* poems.

An entry in the US *Catholic Encyclopaedia* illustrates the effect. Referring to the two *Stabat Mater* versions, it states somewhat fulsomely:

> A large literature has grown about the hymns, Protestants sharing with Catholics a deep, and often glowingly expressed, admiration for its (*sic*) pathos, its vividness of description, its devotional sweetness and unction, its combination of easy rhythmic flow with exquisite double rhyming and finished stanzaic form.[2]

One of a number of the non-Catholic commentators was the Anglican pastor, classical scholar and hymn-writer, Dr John Mason Neale, an expert on early Church hymns. He translated many Greek and Latin prayers and hymns into English, among them the hymn *O come, O come, Emanuel*. He himself composed the Christmas favourite, *Good King Wenceslas*.

His conclusion about the *Stabat Mater* controversy was that both poems were the work of Jacopone. In his view, the similarities between them showed this while the dissimilarities indicated that the *Speciosa* was written when he first started composing and the *Dolorosa* was his later work when he was an accomplished poet.[3]

Another non-Catholic expert disagrees with the opinion that Jacopone was the author of both hymns. He is Dr Philip Schaff, a Swiss Protestant theologian and author of a book on the best religious poems of all ages and tongues published in 1881.[4] His view was that 'the mysterious charm and power of the two hymns are due to the subject.' As regards their authorship, he expressed the view that 'A poet would hardly write a parody on his own poem'.

One of the many non-Catholic translators of both the poems (as well as of *Dies Irae*) was Dr Abraham Coles, an American of British descent.[5] He spoke of the *Dolorosa* as 'powerful in its pathos beyond almost anything that has ever been written.' However, both he and Schaff, while great admirers of Catholic hymns, were strongly critical of what they condemned as their Mariolatry, which they considered heretical. For the same reason, the contemporary Anglican Archbishop of Dublin, Richard Chenevix Trench, omitted them from his book of *Sacred Latin Poetry*, published in 1874.[6]

Even more outspoken on this matter was an American writer, Franklin Johnson. In a book on the *Mater Speciosa* and the *Mater Dolorosa*, he called them 'the two most tender hymns of the Roman Church.' Nevertheless, he added that 'they are disfigured by the gross Mariolatry of the Roman Church, and on this account are unfit for the devotional use of Christians not connected with that sect. I have added adaptations of the hymns in which this objectionable feature will not be found.'[7]

He accomplished his 'adaptations' in his own translations of both hymns by producing two different versions of each. The first, intended for the general reader, was a more faithful translation of the original; the other was for 'the Protestant reader, unfamiliar as he is with ecclesiastical legend and Roman dogmatics.'

This version was given the title of being 'adapted for the devotional use of Protestants.'

The 'adaptations' are made in relatively few lines and are slight but significant. A few examples make the point. In the 'regular' *Speciosa* translation, Mary is addressed as 'Mother, fount of love's devotion'; in the 'adapted' version, she becomes its 'home'; 'Let me feel' becomes 'I would feel' and 'Grant me' becomes 'Teach me'.

In his *Dolorosa* translations, the changes are even more doctrinaire. In the 'regular' version, the poet calls on Mary, in progressively insistent terms, to do things or get things done for him. In the 'adapted' version, he trusts good things will happen and evil be averted and, to this end, he bypasses Mary and deals directly with God the Father and Christ the Son.

The 'regular' text is:

> Virgin, virgins all excelling
> For thy love and grief a dwelling
> Pure and holy make in me
>
> Let me bear Christ's crucifying
> Let me know the pains of dying
> That He suffered on the tree

The 'adapted' version is:

> Jesus, all our thoughts excelling
> For Thy love and grief a dwelling
> Pure and holy make in me
>
> Let me know Thy crucifying
> Let me feel the pains of dying
> Thou didst suffer on the tree[8]

In my view, this latter version has the effect of slowing the tempo and softening the mood of the poem.

On the question of the authorship of the original *Speciosa* and *Dolorosa* poems, Johnson is a strong supporter of the 'common authorship' camp, which holds that Jacopone wrote both. As evidence, he claims that 'the fervour of the hymn, and specially of the tenth stanza, which almost borders upon madness, agrees well with the character of the monk.'[9]

Johnson's own appraisal of both hymns is perceptive:

> In metrical structure they are alike, and much of the language is the same in both. But though they thus resemble each other in external features, they differ in spirit and aim. The first is a paean, the second a dirge; the first is adapted to Christmas, the second to Good Friday; the first contemplates the cradle of Christ, the second His cross; the first rejoices in the birth of the Divine Babe, though its happiness is dashed with tears as it looks from the glad beginning to the tragical end, from Bethlehem to Calvary, from the manger to the tomb, while the second exhibits throughout a heart broken by the anguish of Mary and her Son.[10]

Franklin Johnson, having studied various translations of the Mater Dolorosa, expressed his indebtedness to an English version by the Rev. W. S. McKenzie of Boston. He said McKenzie had been faithful to the Latin in an eminent degree, and his work possessed the merit of a smooth and graceful style. Dr Johnson was a Baptist minister from Ohio, who studied in Germany and travelled in Europe before returning to the United States. Until his retirement in 1908, he was Professor of Church History and Homiletics at the University of Chicago. As an academic, he made many contributions to encyclopaedias and reviews, and published translations of Latin and Anabaptist hymns.

The *Catholic Encyclopaedia* does not come down firmly on one side or the other of the controversy about the authorship of the *Stabat Mater* poems. However, it calls the *Doloroso* and the *Speciosa* 'companion hymns', suggesting that they were both written by the same author. It even speculates, as did Dr John Mason Neale, that the *Speciosa* might have been the poet's work during his apprentice days while the more polished *Dolorosa* was his later work when he had become a master poet.[11]

Apart from infrequent and ambiguous or conflicting comments like these, the *Speciosa* was again largely forgotten until an interesting development in 1952. In that year, a young French scholar and author was researching material for a book he was writing on the Italian Franciscan poets of the thirteenth century. In the Bibliothèque Nationale in Paris he came across a fifteenth-century manuscript containing the *Speciosa* poem.

The young scholar, then only nineteen years of age, was Frédéric Ozanam. Like the Anglican Dr Neale, he was the founder of a religious group. His is more widely known as the Society of St Vincent de Paul, which has since spread all over the world. Ozanam died when he was only forty. Both he and his co-founder, Sister Rosalie Rendu of the Daughters of Charity, were later beatified by Pope John Paul II.[12]

The discovery of the manuscript did not solve the uncertainty about the authorship of the *Speciosa*. Both it and the *Dolorosa* are still baffling the experts about their provenance. Ozanam himself advanced the theory that Jacopone had composed both *Stabats* at the same time and when he was still at the apprentice stage. He tried himself to translate the *Speciosa* into verse but gave up, saying that both poems were 'untranslatable.'[13]

Some of Jacopone's more recent biographers are continuing the argument. George T. Peck rejects the possibility that Jacopone was the *Dolorosa's* author, on the grounds that he had no grasp of Latin or, even if he had, would not use it because St Francis had regarded it as the language of the upper classes.[14]

In contrast, Evelyn Underhill, writing in 1919, has no doubt at all about his authorship. She is even prepared to identify at what stage in his life he wrote it. Basing her judgment on her evaluation of Jacopone's ascetic condition at the time, she opts for a date between his fiftieth and sixtieth years of age (1280 to 1290). These were the years, she says, 'when the thoughts of the Passion certainly engrossed him and his technical powers were at their height.'[15]

Other writers favour a date in the final six years of his life (he died in 1306) when he was living quietly in the Poor Clare house at Collazone.

Whoever was the author of the *Speciosa*, the general consensus of literary historians is that it is not in the same league as the *Dolorosa* in richness of style or degree of intensity. The Latin is more gauche and awkward than it is in the original *Stabat Mater Dolorosa* where, for the most part, it flows freely and sounds natural.

This is not surprising whatever theory about the provenance of the two *Stabat Maters* is accepted. The *Speciosa* was written either by an unskilled apprentice poet, whether or not he was Jacopone, or by an older poet who was comparatively unskilled. If by Jacopone, he was deliberately tarnishing his earlier masterpiece as part of his mystic self-punishment. And if, as I believe, the *Dolorosa* was the first to have been written, then it was by Jacopone at the peak of his powers.

In my view, the *Speciosa* is no masterpiece, especially so in the original Latin. Anyone reading both of the poems one after the other could be forgiven for assuming that the *Dolorosa* is being deliberately stood on its chronological head. As Franklin Johnson noted, the description of Christ's crucifixion is being inverted to apply to his nativity.[16] Mary is no longer weeping for her Son dying on a cross on the hill of Calvary in Jerusalem on the first Good Friday. Instead she is cuddling her newborn child and placing him in the manger in Bethlehem on that first Christmas morning.

The *Speciosa* not only adopts the metre and rhyming arrangement of the *Dolorosa* but also poaches whole lines from it and, even more blatantly, uses them in a way that seems to cock a thumb at the sensitivity and religious sincerity of the original. There is a snide quality to it that no poet would want to be associated with his work and that Latin readers or hearers would justifiably resent.

I have calculated that fourteen of the sixty lines in the *Dolorosa* are repeated word-for-word in the sixty-six lines of the *Speciosa* version while two and three words at a time are 'lifted' (to use a journalistic term) from the remainder. The effect this leaves is that the *Speciosa* poet is straining, as well he might, to find appropriate words to fill the gaps remaining after no more lines or phrases can be 'borrowed' from the original. Either this manipulation is a deliberate effort to mock or trivialise the original poem by holding it up to contempt or, difficult as it may be to believe, a conscious decision by Jacopone himself to devalue his own work as part of his mystic development.

English translations, concentrating on giving a tender and empathetic impression of the Christmas scene, cannot or do not reflect the feeling of awkwardness this creates. I am convinced that the poet would not use one module of his own work to cheapen what is, at least in my opinion, another much more important one. A more likely supposition is that it might rather be the work of an envious fellow poet jeering at the original author or an insensitive one mocking him. The Latin[17] and my English[18] versions of the *Stabat Mater Speciosa* are given here so that readers interested in the controversy about respective ownership can form their own opinion.

Latin Version	D. Fisher Version
1. *Stabat Mater speciosa* *Juxta foenum gaudiosa* *Dum jacebat parvulus*	1. Near the infant's manger smiling Stood the mother so beguiling While her baby slumbered there
2. *Cujus animam gaudentem* *Laetabundam et ferventem* *Pertransivit jubilus*	2. Hers the heart that's so enraptured All the jubilation captured Nothing could her joy impair
3. *O quam laeta et beata* *Fuit ilia immaculata* *Mater unigeniti*	3. Oh how pleased and so elated Was that virgin mother fated To bring forth the Glorious One
4. *Quae gaudebat et ridebat* *Exultabat cum videbat* *Nati partum inclyti*	4. She rejoiced and smiled with pleasure Seeing her distinguished treasure Who was God's illustrious Son
5. *Quisquam est qui non gauderet,* *Christi matrem si videret* *In tanto solatio?*	5. Who could fail to be excited Watching Mary so delighted In such comfort and such joy
6. *Quis non possit collaetari* *Christi matrem contemplari* *Ludentem cum filio?*	6. Who'd not join, one with another Glad to see Christ's darling mother Playing with her infant boy
7. *Pro peccatis sum gentis* *Christum vidit cum jumentis* *Et algori subditum*	7. With the animals beside him And the winter's chill to chide him Christ will save the sin-defiled
8. *Vidit suum dulcem natum* *Vagientem, adoratum* *Vili diversorio*	8. Mary watched her infant babbling Heard her dear one softly prattling Wrapped her cloak around her child
9. *Nato Christo in praesepe* *Coeli cives canunt laete* *Cum immenso gaudio*	9. Heaven's angels laud his glory Heralding the Christmas story In the manger Christ is born

Latin Version	D. Fisher Version
10. *Stabat senex cum puella* *Non cum verbo nec loquela* *Stupescentes cordibus*	10. Elder stands beside the maiden Neither need with words be laden In the wonder of that morn
11. *Eja mater fons amoris* *Me sentire vim ardoris* *Fac ut tecum sentiam;*	11. Mother fount of human feeling Make me sense the power of healing So that I may feel like thee
12. *Fac ut ardeat cor meum* *In amatum Christum Deum* *Ut sibi complaceam*	12. Make my heart be ever burning For the love of Christ be yearning So may I his comfort be
13. *Sancta mater istud agas* *Prone introducas plagas* *Cordi fixas valide*	13. Holy Mother let me languish Let me share the Saviour's anguish In my heart his wounds imbed
14. *Tui nati coelo lapsi* *Jam dignati foeno nasci* *Poenas mecum divide*	14. From above your son descended On the manger's hay transcended Let me suffer in his stead
15. *Fac me vere congaudere* *Jesulino cohaerere* *Donec ego vixero*	15. Let me join his celebration Little Jesus our salvation For as long as I shall live
16. *In me sistat ardor tui* *Puerino fac me frui* *Dum sum in exsilio*	16. In your love my love is sharing For the baby boy we're caring Exiled here my all I give
17. *Virgo virginum praeclara* *Mihi jam non sis amara* *Fac me parvum rapere*	17. Virgin of all virgins splendid With me do not feel offended Let me shield the child from strife
18. *Fac ut pulchrum infantem portem* *Qui nascendo vicit mortem* *Volens vitam tradere*	18. Lovely child on manger lying By his birth he conquered dying Willing to give up his life
19. *Fac me tecum satiari* *Nato me inebriari* *Stantem in tripudio*	19. Love has left us saturated With devotion permeated Standing in is presence here
20. *Inflammatus et accensus* *Obstupescit omnis sensus* *Tali me commercio*	20. Love invades all our defences Love for him pervades our senses Such accord let us hold dear
21. *Fac me nato custodiri* *Verbo Dei praemuniri* *Conservari gratia*	21. Let me have the child's protection And the Holy Book's direction As my worldly race is run
22. *Quando corpus morietur* *Fac ut animae donetur* *Tui nati gloria!*	22. When my requiem is chanted Make sure that my soul be granted All the glory of your Son

The following is the Denis Florence MacCarthy version of the poem which readers may find more sympathetic and emotional than mine.[19]

MacCarthy Version

1. By the crib wherein reposing
with His eyes in slumber closing
lay serene her Infant-boy

2. Stood the beauteous Mother feeling
bliss that could not bear concealing
so her face o'erflowed with joy

3. Oh the rapture naught could smother
of that most Immaculate Mother
of the sole-begotten One

4. When with laughing heart exulting
she beheld her hopes resulting
In the great birth of her Son

5. Who would not with gratulation
see the happy consolation
of Christ's Mother undefiled?

6. Who would not be glad surveying
Christ's dear Mother bending, praying
playing with her heavenly Child

7. For a sinful world's salvation
Christ her Son's humiliation
She beheld and brooded o'er

8. Saw Him weak, a child, a stranger
yet before Him in the manger
kings lie prostrate and adore

9. O'er that lowly manger winging
joyful hosts from heaven were singing
canticles of holy praise

10. While the old man and the maiden
speaking naught, with hearts o'erladen
pondered on God's wondrous ways

11. Fount of love forever flowing
with a burning ardor glowing
make me, Mother, feel like thee

12. Let my heart with graces gifted
all on fire to Christ be lifted
and by Him accepted be

13. Holy Mother deign to bless me
with His sacred Wounds impress me
let them in my heart abide

14. Since He came, thy Son, the Holy
to a birth-place ah, so lowly
all His pains with me divide

15. Make me with true joy delighted
to Child-Jesus be united
while my days of life endure

16. While an exile here sojourning
make my heart like thine be burning
with a love divine and pure

17. Spotless Maid and sinless Woman
make us feel a fire in common
make my heart's long longing sure

18. Virgin of all virgins highest
prayer to thee thou ne'er denyest
let me bear thy sweet Child too

19. Let me bear Him in my bosom
Lord of life and never lose Him
since His birth doth death subdue

20. Let me show forth how immense is
the effect on all my senses
of an union so divine

21. All who in the crib revere Him
like the shepherds watching near Him
will attend Him through the night

22. By thy powerful prayers protected
grant O Queen that His elected
may behold heaven's moving light

23. Make me by His birth be guarded
by God's holy word be warded
by His grace till all is done

24. When my body lies obstructed
make my soul to be conducted
to the vision of thy Son. Amen

Finally, for those interested, here is a literal translation of the *Speciosa* by Hans van der Velden:[20]

1. The beautiful Mother
stood joyously at the crib
in which her child lay

2. Through her exultant soul
Dancing with joy
Went a song of rejoicing

3. O how jubilant and blessed
was the immaculate
Mother of the Only-begotten

4. O how happy and laughing
And exultant did she watch
The birth of her divine Son

5. Who would not rejoice
If he saw the Mother of Christ
In such comfort?

6. Who would not (be) jubilant too
Watching Christ's Mother
Playing with her Son?

7. For the sins of His people
Amidst beasts of burden she saw
Jesus subjected to the cold.

8. She saw her sweet offspring
That she adored crying
Swathed in cheap bandages

8a. For just-born Christ in his crib
The angels sing joyously
And in great rejoicing

8b. The old man stood at his young wife
Without speaking and his heart
Filled with unspeakable wonder

9. Oh Mother fountain of love
Make me feel your ardour
Let me share it with you

10. Make my heart burn
With the love of Christ-God
And find grace in his eyes

11. Blessed Mother, be not harsh
Cause your sufferings
To be fixed deeply in my heart

12. With your child from heaven
Let me share my part
Of the penance He deigns to bear

13a. Make me rejoice with you
and share the adoration of Jesus
as long as I shall live

13b. May your ardour fill me
May the child be my refuge
In my exile

14. Familiarize me with this ardour
Make that I do not turn
From this desire

15. Virgin, most exalted among virgins
Be not bitter towards me
Let me take the child in my arms

16. Let me have the strength of him
Who by his birth conquers death
And is willing to give his life

17. Let me be with you fulfilled
Intoxicated with your first-born
Under such good omens

18. Thus aflame with fire of love
All feelings are silenced
By such selflessness

19. May the first-born protect me
And Christ's word strengthen me
And his blessing save me

20. When my body dies
Then let my soul behold
The sight of your first-born.

Notes

[1]   See H. Henry, 'Stabat Mater' in *The Catholic Encyclopaedia* (New York: Robert Appleton Company, 1912), vol. XIV p. 240.

[2]   *Ibid.*

[3]   See J. M. Neale, *Hymnal Noted* (London: Novello, Ewer and Company, 1851).

[4]   See P. Schaff, & A. Gilman, A., eds., *A Library of Religious Poetry* (London: S. Low, Marston, Searle and Rivington, 1881).

[5]   See A. Coles, *Stabat Mater (Dolorosa)* (New York: D. Appleton and Company, 3rd ed 1891), p. 4.

[6]   See R. C. Trench, *Sacred Latin Poetry* (London: Macmillan and Co., 1874.)

[7]   See F. Johnson, *The Stabat Mater Speciosa and The Stabat Mater Dolorosa* (Boston: D. Lothrop & Company, 1886), pp. 5, 22.

8   *Ibid.*, pp. 33, 37.
9   *Ibid.*, p. 12.
10   *Ibid.*, p. 5.
11   See Henry, 'Stabat Mater', p. 240.
12   See G. Bertrin, 'Antoine-Frédéric Ozanam' in *The Catholic Encyclopaedia* (New York: Robert Appleton Company, 1912), vol. XI, p. 378.
13   See Henry, 'Stabat Mater', p. 240.
14   See G. T. Peck, *The Fool of God* (Alabama: The University of Alabama Press, 1980, p. 150, p. 195, n. 13.
15   See E. Underhill, *Jacopone da Todi, Poet and Mystic* (London: J. M. Dent & Sons, 1919), p. 204.
16   See Johnson, *The Stabat Mater Speciosa and The Stabat Mater Dolorosa*, p. 123.
17   See Chapter 18, p. 141.
18   See Chapter 16, p. 125.
19   See D. F. MacCarthy, *Stabat Mater Speciosa/By The Crib Wherein Reposing* at www.preces-latinae.org/thesaurus/BVM/SMSpeciosa.html.
20   See H. van der Velden, *Stabat Mater Speciosa* at www.stabatmater.info.

25

POSTSCRIPT: FOCAL SCOIR

HOSE READERS WHO have come this far with me may wonder at the title I have given this final chapter. It is not Latin. It is, in fact, an Irish phrase that literally translates as 'departing word' or 'leaving remark'. I use it here because it expresses my feeling that I will soon be unable to continue practising the writing craft I have so enjoyed doing for nearly all of the past 94 years.

Whether anything I have ever written has been of value to anyone is something I shall never know. If anything were, I would wish it to be this book. That is because my purpose in writing it has been to honour Mary by translating a Latin poem that had described her suffering so vividly.

How this simple idea grew into a book was fortuitous. As soon as I had begun to study the poem more diligently than before, I was lured into further searches into different aspects of a topic that had by then caught my closer interest. From there on, as new aspects of the poem came to light, I was more and more deeply absorbed in what became a sort of detective story or a challenging jigsaw puzzle.

To claim that I solved the murder mystery or finished the jigsaw puzzle would be vainglorious. All I have done is to add another voice to those who believe that Jacopone da Todi was the author of the poem and that history, the papacy and some commentators had failed to accord him his rightful place in literature. In doing so, I found it necessary to set him and the *Stabat Mater* story into their historical background.

That involved uncovering as much information as possible about Jacopone's own background, his experiences and, especially, the motivating forces that inspired his religious convictions and writings. In addition, the record had to include a *tour d'horizon*, however sketchy it had to be, of the thirteenth and fourteenth centuries world in which Jacopone lived.

Finally, I found it necessary first to discover and subsequently to explain how the structural differences between the Latin and English languages make it so difficult, if not impossible, to replicate across a 700-year cultural gap, the emotional effect of Jacopone's poem.

It was probably inevitable that I would discount Emeritus Pope Benedict XVI's support for his papal predecessor, Innocent III, and his dismissal of Jacopone da Todi as more likely to be the author of the *Stabat Mater*. Some Popes, past and recent, have had a tendency to endorse their predecessors when it seemed likely to be useful for the Church, as Pope Francis did recently by canonising two of his papal antecedents whose different theological outlooks were splitting Catholicism.

For any kind of papal approval, Benedict would inevitably prefer an erudite theologian like himself rather than an apparently crazy poet who had provoked excommunication and imprisonment. His vote will almost certainly carry enough weight into the future to ensure that the title of Blessed, which, even before his death, the common people of his time had conferred on Jacopone, will never receive Vatican sanction. There will never be a Saint Jacopone.

It is only fair to acknowledge here that, regardless of my own efforts and those of many others to solve its mysteries, many uncertainties regarding the *Stabat Mater* story still persist. While nothing new has happened to throw more light on the question, modern experts on these matters, while not championing Pope Innocent, are now less supportive than before of Jacopone.

The existing viewpoint seems to be that since neither Pope nor poet can definitively be declared the author of the *Stabat Mater Dolorosa* and, consequently, of the *Stabat Mater Speciosa,* both of them should be ruled out and the search continued for the genuine one who has still to be found. The unsolved problems regarding both poems remain.

However, I hope that my readers have by now come to know a good deal more about the *Stabat Mater* than they had previously and that they recognise the value of the work both of its original author and of the translators who brought the English language versions to them.

I leave them with the wish that the Mother of God, whose sufferings on Calvary aroused so much indignation in the poet and so much desire to share them, will take all of us into her care and plead with her son on our behalf to merit the glory of Paradise.

BIBLIOGRAPHY

Scripture quotations are from the ESV® Bible (The Holy Bible, English Standard Version®), copyright © 2001 by Crossway, a publishing ministry of Good News Publishers. Used by permission. All rights reserved. http://biblehub.com/esv/Luke/2.htm

Coles, A., *Stabat Mater (Dolorosa)*. New York: D. Appleton and Company, 3rd ed 1891.

Herberman, C. G., Pace, E. A., Pallen, C. B., Shahan, T. J. & Wynne, J. J., eds, *The Catholic Encyclopaedia*. New York: Robert Appleton Company, 1907–12.

Johnson, F., *The Stabat Mater Speciosa and The Stabat Mater Dolorosa*. Boston: D. Lothrop & Company 1886.

McArthur, T., *The Oxford Companion to the English Language*. Oxford: Oxford University Press, 1992.

Methuen, A. ed, *An Anthology of Modern Verse*. London: Methuen & Co., 26th school edition 1935.

Moore, T., *Moore's Poetical Works*. London: Longman, Brown, Green and Longmans, 1843.

Neale, J. M., *Hymnal Noted*. London: Novello, Ewer and Company, 1851.

Norwich, J. J., *The Popes*. London: Vintage Books, 2012.

Palgrave, F. T., *The Golden Treasury* updated by Press, J. Oxford: Oxford University Press, 6th ed 2002.

Peck, G. T., *The Fool of God*. Alabama: The University of Alabama Press, 1980.

Ricks, C. ed., *The Oxford Book of English Verse*. Oxford: Oxford University Press, 1999.

Schaff, P., and Gilman, A., eds., *A Library of Religious Poetry*. London: S. Low, Marston, Searle and Rivington, 1881.

Schoenbechler, R., 'Stabat Mater' in McKenna, E. ed. *The Collegeville Hymnal* Collegeville, MN.: Liturgical Press, 1990.

Trench, R. C., *Sacred Latin Poetry*. London: Macmillan and Co., 1874.

Tuchman. B., *A Distant Mirror: The Calamitous 14th Century*. New York: Alfred A. Knopf, 1978.

Underhill, E., *Jacopone da Todi, Poet and Mystic*. London: J. M. Dent & Sons, 1919.

World Wide Web pages

Bulman, B. E., *Stabat Mater* at www.warnerclassics.com/downloads/df/5756702.pdf.

Caswall, E., *Stabat Mater* at *Lyra Catholica* New York: E.Dunigan & Brother, 1851 in https://archive.org/stream/lyracatholicacon00newy#page/n5/mode/2up.

Danks, H. P., composer, and Calef, J., 'Won't you Buy my Pretty Flowers?' Horner, J. S., Dayton, OH: 1887 at www.loc.gov/item/ihas.100005388/.

Dante Alighieri, *Paradiso Cantos 1–XXXIV The Divine Comedy* English ed. translated by Henry Wadsworth Longfellow at www.divinecomedy.org/divine_comedy.html.

Heman, F., *Casabianca* reprinted from Holland, R. S. ed., *Historic Poems and Ballads*. Philadelphia: George W. Jacobs & Co., 1912 at www.poetryarchive.com /h/casabianca.html.

ICEL 1973, *The Roman Missal* (translation *Missale Romanum* 1969) prayer for the Jews.

Jacopone da Todi, *Le Laude* in Ferri, G. ed, *Scrittori d'Italia, Iacopone aa Todi, Le Laude*. Laterza: Bari, 1915 at http://www.gutenberg.org/files/29977/29977-8.txt.

Jakobson, R., 'On Linguistic Aspects of Translation' at www.translationdirectory.com/articles/article1667.php.

Jewish History website produced by the Destiny Foundation, Lakewood, NJ at http://www.jewishhistory.org/the-black-death/.

Leip, H. and Schultze N., 'Lili Marlene' at http://lyricsplayground.com/alpha/songs/l/lilimarlene.shtml.

Longfellow, H. W., 'Hiawatha' at www.online-literature.com/henry_longfellow/925.

Luther, M., *The Ninety-Five Theses*, Wittenberg, 1517 at6 http://www.luther.de/en/95thesen.html.

MacCarthy, D. F., A Translation of The 'Stabat Mater' in *The Sacred Heart Review* 35/15 (7 April 1906), p. 242 at http://newspapers.bc.edu Boston College.

MacCarthy, D. F., Stabat Mater Speciosa/By The Crib Wherein Reposing at http://www.preces-latinae.org/thesaurus/BVM/SMSpeciosa.html.

Poe, E. A., 'The Raven' at www.poetry-archive.com/p/the_raven.html.

Roman Catholic Saints, www.roman-catholic-saints.com/blessed-jacopone-of-todi.html.

Stabat Mater in *Graduale Romanum* (Vatican Edition, 1908) at www.ccwatershed.org/media/pdfs/13/07/11/17-23-33 0.pdf Corpus Christi, TX: Corpus Christi Watershed, 2013.

Velden, H. van der, *Stabat Mater* and *Stabat Mater Speciosa* at www.stabatmater.info.

Venuti, L., *Translation Changes Everything* Abingdon: Routledge, 2013 at http://books.google.co.uk.

White, F., 'The Plague, or Black Death, in Ireland', Times Past column in *The Nationalist*, Carlow, 19/11/2014 www.carlow-nationalist.ie/2014/11/21.